BLUEBOOK of ASSEMBLY ROUTINES for the IBM® PC & XT

Assembly language is essential for critical programming tasks such as high-speed graphics, special sound effects, efficient number crunching, and rapid manipulation of text files. However, not all IBM PC programmers are fluent in assembly language; and even for those who are, writing such routines can be a difficult and time-consuming process.

This book presents a large number of highly efficient, prewritten, fully debugged assembly language routines which can be easily plugged into existing IBM PC programs—not only assembly language programs, but BASIC, Pascal, and other languages as well. And you don't need to be an assembly language programmer to use these routines: any programmer can now tap the full power of 8088 assembly language on the IBM PC or XT.

Here you'll find routines to perform ultra high-precision arithmetic, create special type fonts, fill areas of the screen with color, compose special sound effects, search and modify strings, plot points and lines, and alter text files. Many routines actually improve on those built into the IBM PC: the line drawing routine, for example, is three times faster. If you need to "supercharge" your programs, this book will show you how.

Christopher L. Morgan

Christopher L. Morgan is a professor at California State University, Hayward, where he teaches mathematics and computer science, including computer graphics, assembly language programming, computer architecture, and operating systems. Dr. Morgan has given talks and authored papers in pure mathematics and on representations of higher-dimensional objects in computers. He is director of the computer graphics lab at Hayward and is a member of a number of professional associations, including the American Mathematical Society, the National Council of Teachers of Mathematics, and the Association for Computing Machinery. He is coauthor along with Mitchell Waite of *8086/8088 16-Bit Microprocessor Primer* and *Graphics Primer for the IBM PC*.

BLUEBOOK of ASSEMBLY ROUTINES
for the
IBM® PC & XT

by
Christopher L. Morgan

℗

A Plume/Waite Book
New American Library
New York and Scarborough, Ontario

Several trademarks and/or service marks appear in this book. The companies listed below are the owners of the trademarks and/or service marks following their names.

International Business Machines Corporation: IBM, IBM PC, IBM Personal Computer, IBM PC XT, PC-DOS
Microsoft: MS-DOS, MBASIC
Digital Research: CP/M, CP/M-86
MicroPro International Corporation: WordStar
Apple Computer Inc.: Apple
Intel Corporation: Intel
SoftTech Microsystems: UCSD p-System
Epson Corporation: Epson
Atari Inc.: ATARI
Lotus: Lotus 1-2-3
Information Unlimited Software: EasyWriter
ATT Corporation: Bell Laboratories, Unix
ComputerLand
KayPro
Osborne
Xerox Corporation

Library of Congress Cataloging in Publication Data

Morgan, Christopher L.
  Bluebook of assembly routines for the IBM PC & XT.

  "A Plume/Waite book."
  Includes index.
  1. IBM Personal Computer—Programming. 2. IBM Personal Computer XT—Programming. 3. Assembler language (Computer program language) 4. Routines (Computer programs) I. Title.
QA76.8.I2594M64   1984   001.64′2   84-4707
ISBN 0-452-25497-3

PLUME TRADEMARK REG. U.S. PAT. OFF. AND FOREIGN COUNTRIES
REGISTERED TRADEMARK—MARCA REGISTRADA
HECHO EN WESTFORD, MASS., U.S.A.

SIGNET, SIGNET CLASSIC, MENTOR, PLUME, MERIDIAN and NAL BOOKS are published in the United States by New American Library, 1633 Broadway, New York, New York 10019, in Canada by The New American Library of Canada Limited, 81 Mack Avenue, Scarborough, Ontario M1L 1M8

First Printing, May, 1984

1 2 3 4 5 6 7 8 9

Book and cover design by Dan Cooper
Typography by Walker Graphics

PRINTED IN THE UNITED STATES OF AMERICA

Contents

Acknowledgments

There are a number of people I would like to thank for their valuable help in making this book possible.

Mitchell Waite and Robert Lafore at the Waite Group have provided support, encouragement, and guidance as well as feedback which made my job at least an order of magnitude easier.

I thank my wife Carol and my children Betsy and Thomas for their patience as they endured long hours without me while I isolated myself to work on this book.

My graphics students have provided a testing ground for many of the graphics algorithms. Some of these students, including Joe Vierra, Les Withrow, Kathy Munson, Jodi Duprau, and Kathy Colomb, have worked on the fill algorithm which is used in the last program in the graphics chapter.

Preface

This is a book of assembly language routines for the IBM PC and is part of the Plume/Waite Series of IBM PC books. Of the other books in this series we recommend that you also obtain a copy of *Assembly Language Primer for the IBM® PC and XT* by Robert Lafore (New York: Plume/Waite, New American Library, 1984) for a good introduction to IBM PC assembly language.

There are over one hundred routines in this book covering a wide range of areas including input/output, numerical conversion, multidigit arithmetic, graphics, sound, string manipulation, and file manipulation. These are the areas in which it is crucial to have the kind of control over the computer only available through assembly language.

Each chapter begins with a list of the routines that it contains. The list gives both the name and a short description so that you can quickly locate the routine you are looking for. For example, if you need a routine to plot a point on the graphics screen, then you would look at the beginning of the chapter on graphics and find two point-plotting routines, SETPT and XORPT, one to plot a point by overwriting and one to plot a point using the exclusive OR function. If you need more information you can read the introductory material at the beginning of the chapter and you can turn to the routines themselves where you would find headers with full descriptions of the function, input, output, register usage, and other pertinent information.

The routines in this book were chosen for their usefulness to an assembly language programmer or higher level language programmer who requires assembly language routines. Although the routines were not selected for their simplicity, a great deal of effort has been made to make them short, sweet, and easy to understand. The routines have also been optimized for speed and register usage. In particular, special attention has been paid to optimizing the speed of the graphics routines.

The routines have been designed to be easy for you to use. Besides the easy way in which you can locate and discover their vital facts, these routines are designed to be easy to interface with other assembly language routines to form complete programs or to programs written in a higher level language. Chapter 1 describes how this is done and provides several examples. In particular it shows how to use interfacing routines so that you do not have to change a line of code within the routines supplied in this book.

We hope that you will find this book a valuable addition to your programming library.

Introduction

*A*ssembly language is the fastest and most powerful language for programming the IBM PC. However, even for experienced programmers, it can be difficult and time-consuming to write a really efficient assembly-language routine to perform a specific task. And for those whose programming knowledge is confined to higher-level languages such as BASIC and Pascal, writing such assembly-language routines isn't possible at all.

The aim of this book is to make it possible for all programmers, whether they speak assembly language or not, to incorporate fast, efficient assembly-language routines into their programs. The routines in this book will work equally well with assembly-language programs and with higher-level language programs such as BASIC or Pascal.

This book is not meant to be read from cover to cover (unless you are *really* fascinated by assembly language). It is rather a *cookbook*, in which you can look up recipes for solving specific programming problems. Assembly-language programmers can also use the routines as models, or departure points, for developing their own custom routines.

The routines belong to such diverse and important areas as input/output, numeric conversion, multidigit arithmetic, graphics, sound, strings, and file manipulation. These are areas in which direct control over the computer is especially important. Assembly language provides this direct control because it allows you to access the computer's central processor directly, in its own machine language, thus achieving the speed of execution and access to the computer's hardware not possible in higher-level languages.

This first chapter explains who this book is for, what you need to use it, how it is organized, and how to interface the routines to assembly-language programs and to programs written in higher-level languages. Some basic philosophical points are also discussed, such as register usage and why there are no macros in this book. Each subsequent chapter contains routines devoted to a different subject area. This provides a way of organizing the routines in an easy-to-find manner according to the function that the routine is designed to perform.

Whom This Book Is For

This book is designed for beginners and experts alike who are writing assembly language for the IBM PC or related computers, or are writing in high-level languages which do not provide the speed and control over these machines that is available with assembly language.

Assembly-language programmers of the popular Intel 8086 and 8088 processors should note that the IBM PC uses the 8088 microprocessor, which has the same instruction set as the 8086 microprocessor. Thus these routines will also run on the 8086 CPU. (For a complete description of these two chips, see *8086/8088 16-bit Microprocessor Primer* by Christopher L. Morgan and Mitchell Waite [Peterborough: BYTE/McGraw-Hill, 1982].) Many of the routines in succeeding chapters of this book are of a general nature and depend only upon the presence of an 8086/8088 CPU. These include the numeric and string routines which will be of value to any 8086 or 8088 assembly-language programmer.

To use this book effectively you do not need to be an expert in 8088 assembly language, although experts should also find it useful. Beginners and programmers of high-level languages do not need to understand how the routines work, let alone how to write them from scratch. These skills come with experience, some of which can be gained by studying the routines in this book, some of which can be gained by reading books on 8088 assembly language such as *Assembly Language Primer for the IBM PC and XT* by Robert Lafore (New York: Plume/Waite, New American Library, 1984), and some of which must be gained by sitting down and writing your own assembly-language routines.

If you are a beginner or high-level language programmer you can use these routines by combining them with your own programs. You need only understand how to "package" the routines with other routines, how to call them from your programs, and how to pass data back and forth. We will provide examples of these processes later in this chapter. *Assembly Language Primer for the IBM PC and XT* by Robert Lafore, referred to above, also has detailed explanations.

Special Features of This Book

The IBM PC has special graphics and sound equipment. Each of these important areas has a chapter of routines devoted to it. Assembly language provides control over graphics and sound not possible in any higher-level language. This is especially true for graphics, where hundreds of thousands of picture elements have to be quickly changed to make useful and interesting pictures. The routines in chapter 7, the graphics chapter, have been carefully optimized for maximum speed. The graphics and sound routines are specifically designed for the equipment on the IBM PC, but can be modified to work on other graphics and sound equipment.

Many of the routines in this book interface with the PC disk operating system (DOS) supplied by IBM for the IBM PC. We have chosen to use version 2 of this DOS because of its greater power, but many of the routines can be directly used with version 1 of PC DOS as well as with C/PM-86. In particular, the standard I/O routines in chapter 2 use system calls which are available with all three systems.

In chapter 10, the chapter on file manipulation, the routines are designed specifically for the new "file handle" routines available only with PC DOS version 2. These new calls greatly simplify assembly-language programming of disk files, providing facilities that normally have to be developed by the assembly-language programmer. Our routines show how to use these calls to write programs which will perform such useful tasks as saving text files from communications lines to disk.

Version 2 of PC DOS also has *filters*, a Unix-like feature which, among other things, allows an assembly-language programmer to develop and thoroughly test text processing routines in the friendly environment of the keyboard and screen and then, once the worst bugs are out, use these same routines, unmodified, to manipulate disk files. There are several filter routines included in chapter 10. These can be used directly to count and clean files and may be easily modified for your particular needs.

The routines in this book were carefully tested in an environment in which other assembly-language programs called them in ways that thoroughly exercised their various features.

What You Need to Use This Book

To make the most direct use of this book you should have access to an IBM PC or equivalent computer which has the 8088 CPU, at least 64K of user memory, and version 2 of PC DOS or MS DOS. You will also need the IBM Macro Assembler (MASM) or Small Assembler (ASM) for the 8086/8088, distributed by IBM. If you use the Macro Assembler, you will need at least 96K of memory. Both these assemblers use Intel mnemonics for the processor instruction, allow long names (31 characters) as identifiers for variables and labels, and produce relocatable object modules compatible with the IBM linker which is supplied with PC DOS. IBM recommends that you use the Macro Assembler because it supports all features of its manual, but there are a number of additional features, including *macros*, that we will not need.

A screen-oriented text editor would also be helpful, although you can use EDLIN, which comes with the DOS. If you use a screen-oriented editor with the IBM Macro Assembler, you may find yourself running out of space on a single floppy disk — even on a 320K double-sided floppy disk. We found that there was barely enough room on one 320K disk for the operating system, including the hidden files, the command file, the linker, the debugger, the text editor with its overlay files (ours consumed almost 90K bytes), and the Macro Assembler. A second disk was required for the programs.

For the chapter on graphics you will need the IBM PC Color/Graphics Adapter. However, if you are using a different graphics board, then you might be able to modify many of our routines to work on your system.

The chapter on sound requires the built-in speaker and supporting timer circuits which come with the IBM PC. Other "IBM PC compatible" computers may or may not have this setup. You will have to check whether any such computer is truly compatible with the IBM PC in this regard.

How This Book Is Organized

Each chapter, starting with chapter 2, begins with a short introduction which explains the scope, purpose, and special requirements of the routines included therein. The routines themselves then follow the chapter introduction.

Each routine is carefully documented with a special header which gives the function of the routine, its input, its output, the register usage, the segment usage, other routines called by it, and any special notes. This is considered good programming practice and is required in some form by many companies that use computers. You may not want to include all this information in your program because it takes up space in your source file and requires time and effort to type in. However, it is good to have it somewhere, and so you may want to refer to this book as part of the documentation for your programs.

The source code for each program follows the header. The first line of source code is almost always a PROC instruction. This is short for PROCedure. Each 8088 routine is considered to belong to a larger class of programming structures called *procedures*. In general, procedures are blocks of code which are designed to accomplish a specific task. Procedures can be CALLed as in the case of our routines or they can be inserted "in line" as in the case of macros. The PROC instruction is required by the IBM PC assembler to determine the proper machine code for calling the routine from other routines (whether they are near or far CALLs or RETurns). The last line of source code of any IBM PC assembly procedure is an ENDP (END Procedure) instruction. This tells the assembler exactly what parts of the code (especially all the RETurn instructions) are *in* the procedure. Having such clear beginning and ending statements enforces a modern block structure on assembly language, thus providing the benefits of modern structured programming practices. These practices are designed to, and in fact, do increase the efficiency of those who design, program, and maintain software.

Within the body of each routine we have commented on almost every line to explain its purpose, although some comments such as "save registers" refer to several lines of code and appear only on the first such line. Liberal use has been made of open space. In particular, blank lines (with only a single semicolon) are used to physically divide the routine into small blocks of logically related lines of code, thus making the code easier to read. Code that is easier to read is easier to debug or get right in the first place.

The routines are arranged in order according to how they reference one another. Just as in Pascal, each routine comes before all others which call it. This simplifies the job that the assembler has to do and produces more efficient code. It is also a natural and modern way of organizing programs. This means to you as a user that to understand and implement any particular routine, you need consider only those routines before it.

The order of the chapters is organized in a similar way, starting with basic input/output in chapter 2, then numerical conversion in chapters 3 (binary), 4 (BCD), and 5 (floating point). These first few chapters establish the necessary tools for getting textual and numeric information into and out of the computer, a prerequisite for doing almost any other kind of programming. Chapter 6, Multidigit Arithmetic, contains routines which perform the four basic numerical operations to any desired degree of precision (to the limits determined by the size of the computer's memory). Chapters 7 and 8 cover graphics and sound, respectively, as discussed above. Chapter 9 contains routines to manipulate strings, and chapter 10 contains routines to manipulate files (see the above discussion on files).

Interfacing the Routines to Assembly Language

For the routines in this book to be useful they must be combined with other routines to form complete programs. This can be done entirely in assembly language or in combination with higher-level languages. We'll first see how to work entirely within assembly language; later we'll discuss how these routines may be combined with programs written in higher-level languages such as BASIC. Before launching into our examples we will begin with a preliminary review of *memory segmentation*.

Segment Usage

When programming the 8088 microprocessor in assembly language it is essential to have some knowledge of segments. Segmentation is explained in *8086/8088 16-bit Microprocessor Primer* by Christopher L. Morgan and Mitchell Waite (Peterborough: BYTE/McGraw-Hill, 1982) and the *Assembly Language Primer for the IBM PC and XT* by Robert Lafore (New York: Plume/Waite, New American Library, 1984). In particular, the *Assembly Language Primer for the IBM PC and XT* introduces the ideas behind providing the proper packaging for routines in relation to the segments they use.

The 8088 processor accesses main memory in 64K stretches called *segments*. There are four registers called segment registers which specify the beginning of each of these segments in the one megabyte addressing space of the 8088 CPU. Thus only four segments are active at any one time.

The four segment registers are named CS (Code Segment), SS (Stack Segment), DS (Data Segment), and ES (Extra Segment). Their names indicate their functions. That is, the code segment is used to store processor instructions, the stack segment is used to store the stack, and the data segment is used to store the variables and other data. The extra segment is also used to store data.

When the IP (Instruction Pointer) is used to access memory, it is fetching CPU instructions and therefore is pointing to an address within the code segment. Other addressing registers such as BX and SI normally point to addresses within the data segment, and still others, namely SP and BP, point to addresses within the stack segment. The extra segment is the default segment for DI during string operations (see Figure 1-1 below).

If many assembly-language files are linked together, the various segments will combine and relate to each other in different ways, taking on different personalities. In particular, code segments in different assembly files are most often kept separate and are put in separate areas of memory. The routines in one code segment can easily call routines in other segments via FAR CALLs (no FAR JuMPs, please). There is only a moderate amount of overhead involved in making such switches from one code segment to another, and it is mostly taken care of by the assembler.

The stack segment need only be included in one assembly-language module of the entire program. It should be declared as "STACK" so that the operating system can automatically initialize it as the stack for your

Regular registers	Segment registers			
	CS	SS	DS	ES
IP	Yes	No	No	No
SP	No	Yes	No	No
BP	Yes with override	Default	Yes with override	Yes with override
BX	Yes with override	Yes with override	Default	Yes with override
SI	Yes with override	Yes with override	Default	Yes with override
DI	Yes with override	Yes with override	Default for nonstring operations	Default for string operations

Figure 1.1.   Segment register usage

program. Just before running the program, the operating system automatically sets the stack segment register to point to the beginning of this segment and the stack pointer to point to the end of this segment. While the program runs, the stack grows downward into the body of this segment.

Data segments can be handled differently. In fact, for most programs you only need one data segment which is shared by all the assembly modules. This is easy to arrange – just assign the same name to the data segment in each assembly module and declare each one PUBLIC. The result is one big data segment which contains parts from the various assembly modules. Having just one data segment in the program cuts down on the segment switching overhead required to access the data while the program runs. Having data in its own segment rather than in the code segment is a basic philosophical concept with a great deal of merit. It is another example of the modern structured programming which encourages "modular" design with everything in its own place. In addition, with only 64K bytes per segment, having data in its own separate segment gives a lot more room for the code in the code segment.

With this arrangement, the offset for any particular piece of data is not known at assembly time, but rather only after all the modules have been linked together. As a result, the OFFSET operator, which is an assembler command function, cannot return the correct value of the offset within an entire data segment which stretches over several assembly modules. There is, however, a CPU instruction LEA (Load Effective Address) which loads a specified register with the offset of a specified variable when the program is actually running. This CPU instruction **must** be used instead of the OFFSET operator when you need to compute addresses of variables such as messages and complex data structures.

The extra segment has a number of functions. For example, it can be identified with the data segment, it can be a special area of memory in which data for the operating system is stored, or it can contain special memory such as the video RAM. You can observe how it is used in our routines.

Two Methods of Interfacing to Other Programs

The routines in this book can be combined with other assembly-language programs at the source code level, using a text editor, or they can be put in groups housed in separate assembly-language files and then later *linked* together with other routines, including ones that you write. Combinations of these two methods are also possible.

Combining Routines Within the Same File

Below we have included an example of an assembly-language program entirely contained in one file. It combines several standard I/O routines in chapter 2 with a main program which allows you to interactively select and print messages. It is not designed to be useful itself, but rather to provide a model of how to write a simple, but complete assembly-language module.

```
; EXAMPLE PROGRAM 1
;
;--------------------- equates begin ------------------------------+
cr      equ     13              ; carriage return
lf      equ     1Ø              ; linefeed
;--------------------- equates end --------------------------------+
;
;
;--------------------- stack area begins --------------------------+
stacks  segment stack           ; stack segment starts here
        dw      5 dup(Ø)        ; reserve 5 levels of stack with zeros
stacks  ends                    ; stack segment ends here
;--------------------- stack area ends ----------------------------+
;
;
;--------------------- data area begins ---------------------------+
datas   segment public          ; data segment starts here
;
; MESSAGES
menu    db      cr,lf,'Message Demonstration Program',cr,lf
        db      cr,lf,'Press 1 or 2 for messages or CTRL/C to stop:'
        db      Ø
mess1   db      cr,lf,'message number one',cr,lf,Ø
mess2   db      cr,lf,'message number two',cr,lf,Ø
mess3   db      cr,lf,'You hit an invalid key',cr,lf,Ø
;
datas   ends                    ; data segment ends here
;--------------------- data area ends -----------------------------+
;
;--------------------- code area starts ---------------------------+
codes   segment
;
        assume  cs:codes,ss:stacks,ds:datas
;--------------------- routine begins -----------------------------+
; ROUTINE FOR STANDARD INPUT WITH ECHO
;
stdin   proc    far
        mov     ah,1            ; standard input
        int     21h             ; DOS call
        ret                     ; return
stdin   endp
;--------------------- routine ends -------------------------------+
```

```
;---------------------- routine begins ----------------------------+
;  ROUTINE FOR STANDARD OUTPUT
;
stdout  proc    far
        push    dx              ; save registers
;
        mov     dl,al           ; in DL for DOS call
        mov     ah,2            ; standard output
        int     21h             ; DOS call
;
        pop     dx              ; restore registers
        ret                     ; return
stdout  endp
;---------------------- routine ends ------------------------------+
;
;---------------------- routine begins ----------------------------+
;  ROUTINE TO SEND MESSAGE TO STANDARD OUTPUT
;
stdmessout      proc    far
        push    si              ; save registers
        push    ax
;
stdmessout1:
        mov     al,[si]         ; get byte
        inc     si              ; point to next byte
        cmp     al,Ø            ; done?
        je      stdmessoutexit  ; if so exit
        call    stdout          ; send it out
        jmp     stdmessout1     ; loop for more
;
stdmessoutexit:
        pop     ax              ; restore registers
        pop     si
        ret                     ; return
stdmessout      endp
;---------------------- routine ends ------------------------------+
;
;---------------------- main program begins ----------------------+
;  PROGRAM TO INTERACTIVELY DISPLAY MESSAGES
;
main    proc    far
;
start:
        mov     ax,datas        ; get data segment
        mov     ds,ax           ; put into DS
```

```
ainØ:
        lea     si,menu         ; point to menu message
        call    stdmessout      ; send the message

        call    stdin           ; get key from user
ain1:
        cmp     al,'1'          ; message number 1?
        jne     main2           ; skip if not
        lea     si,mess1        ; point to message 1
        call    stdmessout      ; send the message
        jmp     main4           ; exit to bottom of loop
ain2:
        cmp     al,'2'          ; message number 2?
        jne     main3           ; skip if not
        lea     si,mess2        ; point to message 2
        call    stdmessout      ; send the message
        jmp     main4           ; exit to bottom of loop
ain3:
        lea     si,mess3        ; point to message 3
        call    stdmessout      ; send the message

ain4:
        jmp     mainØ           ; another message?

ain     endp
---------------------- main program ends -------------------------+
odes    ends
---------------------- code area ends ----------------------------+
        end     start
```

We have put everything needed to execute the program in one file or
module called CH1EX1.ASM. You can see that various major components
within this module are in sections delimited by dashed lines with
centered labels which announce the beginning or end of each section.

The first section contains equates. Here is where names are given to
constants which are used in the rest of the program. It is important to
place all equates first because they are referenced by the assembler while
it assembles the rest of the program.

Another reason for placing equates first is that many assembly-
language programs can be made to work in a new environment simply by
changing equates. If the equates are right up front and properly
documented, then programmers who are in charge of integrating various
assembly programs into working systems can do their work much more
efficiently.

The next section contains the stack which is housed in a stack
segment called "STACKS". Notice that we have given this segment the

attribute "STACK". As explained above, the operating system uses this attribute to know where to set up the stack segment register and stack pointer just before the program is run. For this simple program we have reserved five levels (words) of stack. Other programs may require much more.

The data section is next. It is housed in a data segment called "DATAS". The data segment contains all variables and messages. Conforming to our normal practice, we have declared this segment as "PUBLIC" so that it can be accessed by all other parts of the program (if there are any) and can be merged with other data segments in other modules (again, if there are any).

The last few sections contain the code. All code is in one segment called "CODES". Code for each routine is in its own subsection, delimited by dashed lines. The routines are ordered so that each routine is placed before any others which call it. In particular, the main program is last.

Although these routines have headers with detailed descriptions of their function, input, output, register usage, and so on when they are "officially" listed in chapter 2, we have removed the headers from the routines when they appear in programs in this chapter to save space.

Since the main program is an endless loop, we do not need special provisions for returning to the operating system. At any time while this program is running, you can easily return to the operating system by hitting a ⌈Ctrl⌋ C.

The program demonstrates how to use the STDIN and STDMESSOUT routines in chapter 2. It uses the STDIN routine to sense which message you want and the STDMESSOUT routine to display the specified message. The control structure of this program, in which a series of possibilities is checked and possibly performed, can be used to make programs which interact with the user to perform useful work.

Assembling Our Example

Normally, you would put your programming tools, such as editors, assemblers, and linkers on drive A and the assembly language programs that you are developing on drive B.

Under these conditions, to assemble the above program, you type:

```
A>MASM B: CH1EX1;
```

You will get a file called CH1EX1.OBJ on drive B. You will still need to link this before you can run the program. This is accomplished by typing:

```
A>LINK B:CH1EX1;
```

The file CH1EX1.EXE will result. It can now be run with the command:

```
A>B:CH1EX1
```

The program will then sign on, ready to work for you.

Using Separate Files

If you use separate files to house the routines from this book, you will edit and then assemble a number of files separately. Each such file should contain a group of related routines. For example, all routines from a certain chapter might be placed in the same file. Each file then forms a separate assembly *module* for a particular function. That is, all arithmetic routines are in one large file, all graphics in another, and so on. Working in modules like this has advantages in the development process because it cuts down on the time required to edit and assemble code. Code that is already working can be kept in modules which are assembled in final, compact, object code form, while code that is not working is edited and reassembled until it is correct. Each time that the program is tested, the various object code modules are linked together using the *linker* supplied with the DOS.

Routines in one module which are called by routines in other modules must be declared *PUBLIC* within their own assembly-language file and defined as *EXTERNal* in the file containing the routines which called them. These assembler instructions are described in chapter 5 of the *IBM Personal Computer Macro Assembly Language* manual.

Below we have included an example of how this works. It is, in fact, essentially the same program as in our first example, but organized in a different manner.

Let's look at the file containing the main program first. It is called CH1EX2.ASM. It contains most of the same sections as before, including the equates, the stack, the data, and the code. This time, however, there is a section of external references. This is needed because certain subroutines are now missing from the main program module because they are housed in their own module. If you don't declare them to be external, the assembler will think that you forgot them and will give you a whole bunch of serious errors.

```
;  EXAMPLE PROGRAM 2
;
;---------------------- equates begin ----------------------------+
cr      equ     13              ; carriage return
lf      equ     1Ø              ; linefeed
;---------------------- equates end ------------------------------+
;
;+++++++++++++++++++++++ externals begin +++++++++++++++++++++++++++++
        extrn   stdin:far,stdout:far,stdmessout:far
;+++++++++++++++++++++++ externals end +++++++++++++++++++++++++++++++
;
;---------------------- stack area begins ------------------------+
stacks  segment stack           ; stack segment starts here
        dw      5 dup(Ø)·        ; reserve 5 levels of stack with zeros
stacks  ends                    ; stack segment ends here
;---------------------- stack area ends --------------------------+
;
;---------------------- data area begins -------------------------+
datas   segment public          ; data segment starts here
;
;  MESSAGES
menu    db      cr,lf,'Message Demonstration Program',cr,lf
        db      cr,lf,'Press 1 or 2 for messages or CTRL/C to stop:'
        db      Ø
mess1   db      cr,lf,'message number one',cr,lf,Ø
mess2   db      cr,lf,'message number two',cr,lf,Ø
mess3   db      cr,lf,'You hit an invalid key',cr,lf,Ø
;
datas   ends                    ; data segment ends here
;---------------------- data area ends ---------------------------+
;
;---------------------- code area starts -------------------------+
codes   segment
;
        assume  cs:codes,ss:stacks,ds:datas
;---------------------- main program begins ----------------------+
;  PROGRAM TO INTERACTIVELY DISPLAY MESSAGES
;
main    proc    far
;
start:
        mov     ax,datas        ; get data segment
        mov     ds,ax           ; put into DS
;
mainØ:
        lea     si,menu         ; point to menu message
        call    stdmessout      ; send the message
```

```
        call    stdin           ; get key from user
ain1:
        cmp     al,'1'          ; message number 1?
        jne     main2           ; skip if not
        lea     si,mess1        ; point to message 1
        call    stdmessout      ; send the message
        jmp     main4           ; exit to bottom of loop
ain2:
        cmp     al,'2'          ; message number 2?
        jne     main3           ; skip if not
        lea     si,mess2        ; point to message 2
        call    stdmessout      ; send the message
        jmp     main4           ; exit to bottom of loop
ain3:
        lea     si,mess3        ; point to message 3
        call    stdmessout      ; send the message

ain4:
        jmp     main0           ; another message?

ain     endp
---------------------- main program ends ---------------------------+
odes    ends
---------------------- code area ends ------------------------------+
        end     start
```

Each external reference gives the name of a routine or a variable that is not present, and assigns a "type" to it. The type is an essential ingredient in determining the proper machine code for referencing the routine or variable. Thus the type must be declared. Since these routines are in their own separate code segment, they are of type "far" and require "far" CALLs in machine language.

In our example the file CH1IO.ASM contains the subroutines. By examining this module (below), you can see exactly what is needed to package routines in general. Specifically, notice that all the routines are housed in a segment called "CODES". This is not public and will not be combined with segments by that name in other modules.

```
EXAMPLE PROGRAM 3 - I/O MODULE - FILE CH1IO.ASM

---------------------- code area starts ----------------------------+
odes    segment

++++++++++++++++++++++ public declarations start +++++++++++++++++++++
        public  stdin,stdout,stdmessout
++++++++++++++++++++++ public declarations end +++++++++++++++++++++++
```

```
;
        assume  cs:codes
;---------------------- routine begins ----------------------------+
; ROUTINE FOR STANDARD INPUT WITH ECHO
;
stdin   proc    far
        mov     ah,1            ; standard input
        int     21h             ; DOS call
        ret                     ; return
stdin   endp
;---------------------- routine ends ------------------------------+
;
;---------------------- routine begins ----------------------------+
; ROUTINE FOR STANDARD OUTPUT
;
stdout  proc    far
        push    dx              ; save registers
;
        mov     dl,al           ; in DL for DOS call
        mov     ah,2            ; standard output
        int     21h             ; DOS call
;
        pop     dx              ; restore registers
        ret                     ; return
stdout  endp
;---------------------- routine ends ------------------------------+
;
;---------------------- routine begins ----------------------------+
; ROUTINE TO SEND MESSAGE TO STANDARD OUTPUT
;
stdmessout      proc    far
        push    si              ; save registers
        push    ax
;
stdmessout1:
        mov     al,[si]         ; get byte
        inc     si              ; point to next byte
        cmp     al,0            ; done?
        je      stdmessoutexit  ; if so exit
        call    stdout          ; send it out
        jmp     stdmessout1     ; loop for more
;
stdmessoutexit:
        pop     ax              ; restore registers
        pop     si
        ret                     ; return
stdmessout      endp
;---------------------- routine ends ------------------------------+
codes   ends
;---------------------- code area ends ----------------------------+
        end
```

Within the code module are public declarations. We do not have to explicitly declare the type because it is already known from context. That is, the routines and variables are in the module in which the "PUBLIC" command occurs, and so their type is already well known by the assembler.

The routines appear just as they do in the text of chapter 2, except that, again, headers are omitted to conserve space.

To assemble this program you would first enter:

```
>MASM B:CH1EX2;
```

to assemble your main program, and then

```
>MASM B:CH1IO;
```

to assemble your I/O module. You would now have files CH1EX2.OBJ and CH1IO.OBJ on drive B. You would then link these together with the command:

```
>LINK B:CH1EX2 B:CH1IO;
```

To run the program, just type:

```
>B:CH1EX2
```

You should get the same results as before.

nterfacing the Routines to BASIC

The next example demonstrates how to interface routines in this book with BASIC via the CALL statement.

This example is housed in the file CH1EX3.ASM. It converts internal 16-bit integers to ASCII binary form on the display screen using the BIN16OUT routine in chapter 3 of this book.

```
EXAMPLE PROGRAM 4

---------------------- externals begin  ----------------------------+
      extrn    stdout:far
---------------------- externals end   ----------------------------+
```

```
;----------------------- code area starts ---------------------------+
codes    segment
;
         assume  cs:codes
;----------------------- routine begins -----------------------------+
; ROUTINE TO CONVERT FROM INTERNAL 16-BIT BINARY TO ASCII BINARY
;
bin16out         proc    far
;
; a binary number is in DX
;
         push    cx              ; save registers
;
         mov     cx,16           ; loop for a count of 16
bin16out1:
         rol     dx,1            ; rotate DX left once
         mov     al,dl           ; move into AL
         and     al,1            ; just keep digit
         add     al,30h          ; add 30h to AL
         call    stdout          ; send it out
         loop    bin16out1
;
         pop     cx              ; restore registers
         ret                     ; return
;
bin16out         endp
;----------------------- routine ends -------------------------------+
;
;----------------------- main program begins ------------------------+
; PROGRAM TO INTERFACE BETWEEN BASIC AND ASSEMBLY LANGUAGE
;
main     proc    far
;
start:
         push    bp              ; save BP register
         mov     bp,sp           ; point BP to stack
;
         mov     bx,[bp+6]       ; get address of data
         mov     dx,[bx]         ; get the data
         call    bin16out        ; convert to binary
;
         pop     bp              ; restore BP
         ret     2               ; return skipping the data
main     endp
;----------------------- main program ends --------------------------+
codes    ends
;----------------------- code area ends -----------------------------+
         end     start
```

The main part of this program is an interfacing routine which is called by the CALL statement in BASIC. You can use the USR function, but the CALL statement is more flexible and powerful. The interfacing program would be quite different if you used USR. See the *Assembly Language Primer for the IBM PC and XT* by Robert Lafore for an example of that case.

When BASIC's CALL is used, as in our example, data is passed to and from the subroutine via the 8088's system stack. Since the stack is also used to store the return address, special care is needed to grab the right data and not destroy or lose the return address. The BP (Base Pointer) is very handy to assist in this process. Both the Stack Pointer (SP) and the Base Pointer normally point into the stack segment. However, the Stack Pointer cannot be used for the usual addressing modes. The normal practice is to push the contents of the BP onto the stack, move the contents of the SP to the BP, and then use the BP to point to the data. With BASIC, the address of the data, not the actual value of the data, is placed on the stack. Passing the address rather than the value is a tried and true method with a number of important advantages which we won't go into here (but again, see the *Assembly Language Primer*).

Our example shows how the BP is used to access the data (also see Figure 1-2). You can see that at the beginning of the main program, the BP is pushed on the stack and the contents of the SP are moved to the BP. Next, notice how indirect addressing with displacement is used to get

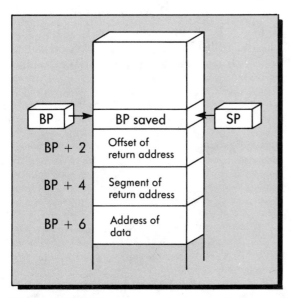

Figure 1-2. Using the stack to pass data to and from BASIC

the address of the single parameter into BX. This is done with the instruction:

```
mov    bx, [bp+6]
```

The displacement of 6 is determined as follows. Two bytes are required to save the BP, two bytes to store the segment of the return address, and two bytes to store the offset of the return address. That's 6 bytes altogether. The address of the last (in this case only) parameter is the very next item on the stack and thus has this displacement. The *IBM Personal Computer BASIC* manual gives formulas for computing the displacements when more variables are involved.

Since the addresses of the parameters are on the stack, one more step is needed to get the data. The instruction:

```
mov   dx, [bx]
```

puts the actual value of the data into DX. From there, a call is made to the BIN16OUT routine to do the work. To return to BASIC, the BP is restored and a special form of the RETurn instruction is used in which a displacement is given. This displacement allows the SP to skip over the data after the return address is POPed from the stack. The displacement is just the number of bytes of the stack used by the data. In this case, one parameter uses one word which is two bytes. Thus the displacement is two.

Notice that by using an interfacing routine we have arranged it so that the routines themselves do not have to be modified to be interfaced to a higher-level language. That is, the routines in this book are general purpose and independent of which high-level (or low-level) language calls them.

It is instructive to look at the BASIC program which calls this assembly-language program:

```
100 ' Test Program for Chapter 1
110 '
120   DEF SEG=&H1F94
130   BINOUT = &H15
140 '
150 ' get the number
160   INPUT "type a number";X%
170 '
```

```
18Ø ' print the number
19Ø    CALL BINOUT(X%)
2ØØ    PRINT
21Ø '
22Ø    GOTO 15Ø
```

On lines 120 and 130, the location (segment and offset) of the assembly-language module is specified. These values are determined by the following procedure: the assembly-language file is assembled with the command:

```
A>MASM B:CH1EX3;
```

then linked with the command:

```
A>LINK CH1EX3 CH1IO/HIGH;
```

The option /HIGH forces the code to be located near the top of available memory away from BASIC. The code is then loaded into memory with the command:

```
A>DEBUG CH1EX3.EXE
```

The R command is next used to display the contents of the registers. The CS register gives the segment address (in this case 1F94 hex) and the IP register gives the offset (in this case 15 hex). BASIC can then be loaded from within DEBUG with the following sequence of commands:

```
-NBASIC
```

```
-L
```

```
-G
```

The first command tells the debug program what file is required, the second command loads it, and the third command executes it.

The BASIC program can be either loaded or written and then run as usual. The *Assembly Language Primer for the IBM PC and XT* explains this process in more detail.

The BASIC program is a simple endless loop which allows the user to input a number in decimal form and then calls our assembly-language program to output this number in binary.

Some Philosophical Notes

Below is an explanation of register usage and a comparison of macros and subroutines.

Register Usage

Each 8088 register has a particular personality. We have been very careful to respect these personality differences. For example, AX is used as a temporary holding bin for data and to hold data for many of the arithmetic and string operations; CX is used as a count register; DX is used as a more permanent place for storing data; BX is used most frequently to compute and hold addresses, but can also hold data; and SI and DI are used to point to indexed data such as strings or arrays (with SI as the source and DI as the destination).

Using CX properly presents interesting problems. Often there are counting loops within counting loops. Both the inner and outer loops should use CX for the count. But how is this done? The secret is using the stack to PUSH and POP the count before and after the body of each loop (see below).

```
            mov     cx,outerloopcount    ; get outer count
outerloop:                               ; top of outer loop
            push    cx                   ; save outer count
            .......                       ; outer code goes here
            .......

;
            mov     cx,innerloopcount    ; get inner count
innerloop:                               ; top of inner loop
            push    cx                   ; save inner count
            .......                       ; inner code goes here
            pop     cx                   ; restore inner count
            loop    innerloop            ; bottom of inner loop
;
            .......                       ; more outer loop code
            pop     cx                   ; restore outer count
            loop    outerloop            ; bottom of outer loop
```

This way, the nesting of the loops corresponds directly to the nesting of the PUSHes and POPs which save the counts for the loop. This idea can be extended to any number of nesting levels and has the added benefit that the code within the inner loop can be freed to use CX as desired.

This advantage outweighs the loss of speed due to the extra overhead of the PUSH and POP instructions.

Macros

What is a "macro" and why are there no macros in this book of assembly-language subroutines?

A macro is a way of taking an often-used section of program code and giving it a name so that the entire section of code need not be written out each time it occurs in the program. Macros are somewhat like subroutines ("procedures") in that the assembly language for both is written as a separate block of code. However, the two differ in the way they are structured when translated into machine language. In the case of macros, the machine language is inserted into the program where it is needed. In the case of subroutines, a CALL is all that appears at the desired location and the machine code resides in its own place in memory.

Macros have certain advantages and disadvantages over subroutines. One important advantage is that they avoid the overhead of the CALLs and RETurn instructions. These take time to execute. However, since the machine code is actually inserted in place, more space in memory will be needed for a program using a macro.

We have not used macros in this book for a number of reasons. The main reason is that they create an additional layer of complexity which hides the very details we wish to display. In extreme cases the assembly code consists of a list of names of macros with hardly any CPU instructions, thus turning the assembly language into some sort of higher-level language. To understand such a program you would have to know what each macro does. It is possible to produce very elegant-looking programs with this approach, but we believe that it is more appropriate for this book to take a straightforward approach in which almost every line of assembly-language source code corresponds directly to a CPU instruction in machine code. However, you might want to "macroize" our code at some point later on as you use it.

2

Input/Output

*T*he routines in this chapter perform fundamental input/output functions for the keyboard, screen, and communications lines. Input/ouput routines are important in assembly language because they not only provide an efficient way to pass data in and out of programs written entirely in assembly language, but also provide excellent control in interfacing the computer with the outside world when higher-level languages are used.

The first eight routines are designated as **standard input/output** and can be used in general-purpose ways to access various I/O devices. The last five routines are special purpose, designed just for the communications lines.

The standard input/output routines in this chapter are implemented with simple DOS calls which normally perform basic keyboard and screen I/O functions. The DOS calls used by these routines are common to versions 1 and 2 of IBM PC DOS and, with one exception (DOS Call 8,

Console input without echo), CP/M-86 as well. However, a word of warning is in order – CP/M-86 makes its DOS calls in a different way than PC DOS does. CP/M-86 uses different registers for input and output and a different interrupt for the system call.

Starting with IBM PC DOS 2, the basic keyboard and screen DOS calls can be *redirected*, and hence our standard input/output routines also enjoy this property. This means that when the standard I/O routines are incorporated in programs that act as DOS commands, then you can get/send the input and/or output through whatever device you want by adding straightforward instructions to the command lines which call these programs. For example, a program can be written (using our keyboard and screen routines) to accept input from the keyboard and send output to the screen, and then later, by redirecting the I/O, it can be used to manipulate disk files. This provides a very powerful programming tool in which the functions performed by a program can be developed independent of I/O considerations.

Special routines for the serial communications lines are included because the routines in the DOS and even in the BIOS are not complete and have certain problems. In particular, we needed a routine (COMINCK) which checks for but does not wait for input from a communications line. This routine is written as a primitive, without reference to any DOS or BIOS calls, because the primitive BIOS input routine for the communications line sometimes scrambles incoming bytes from other computers. This is because it inappropriately changes a handshaking signal (RTS, Request To Send on pin 4 of the RS-232C communications connector). For this same reason, special routines COMON and COMOFF are included to control the appropriate handshaking signal (DTR, Data Terminal Ready on pin 20 of the RS-232C communications lines). These communication routines are required for file manipulation in chapter 10.

STDIN

Standard Input with Echo

Function:　This routine accepts input from the standard I/O device.

Input:　This routine waits for one character code from the standard input device.

Output:　ASCII codes are returned in the AL register. Each character is echoed out the standard output device as it is input through the standard input device.

Registers Used:　AH is modified. AL is used for output.

Segments Referenced:　None

Routines Called:　DOS call number 1 (Keyboard input) is used.

Special Notes:　None

```
; ROUTINE FOR STANDARD INPUT WITH ECHO
;
stdin   proc    far
        mov     ah,1         ; standard input
        int     21h          ; DOS call
        ret                  ; return
stdin   endp
```

STDINNE

Standard Input with No Echo

Function: This routine accepts input from the standard I/O device. No echo is generated.

Input: This routine waits for one character code from the standard input device.

Output: ASCII codes are returned in the AL register. Each character is echoed out the standard output device as it is input through the standard input device.

Registers Used: AH is modified. AL is used for output.

Segments Referenced: None

Routines Called: DOS call number 8 (Console input without echo) is used.

Special Notes: None

```
; ROUTINE FOR STANDARD INPUT WITH ECHO
;
stdinne proc    far
        mov     ah,8            ; standard input without echo
        int     21h             ; DOS call
        ret                     ; return
stdinne endp
```

STDINCK

Standard Input Check

Function: This routine checks, but does not wait for input from the standard I/O device.

Input: Input is from the standard I/O device. No check is made for Ctrl Break.

Output: If a character is available, the routine returns with the flag condition NZ and the character in AL, but if no character is available then the routine returns with the flag condition Z, and AL is meaningless. No echo generated for the input characters.

Registers Used: AH is modified. AL is used for output.

Segments Referenced: None

Routines Called: DOS call number 06h (Direct console I/O) is used.

Special Notes: None

```
; ROUTINE TO CHECK FOR STANDARD INPUT
;
stdinck proc    far
        push    dx              ; save registers
;
        mov     dl,0FFh         ; direct console input
        mov     ah,06h          ; check standard direct input status
        int     21h             ; DOS call
;
        pop     dx              ; restore registers
        ret                     ; return
stdinck endp
```

STDOUT

Standard Output

Function: This routine sends individual characters out the standard output device.

Input: Upon entry an ASCII code is in AL.

Output: A single character is output through the standard output device.

Registers Used: AH is modified. AL is used for input.

Segments Referenced: None

Routines Called: DOS call number 2 (Display output) is used.

Special Notes: None

```
; ROUTINE FOR STANDARD OUTPUT
;
stdout  proc    far
        push    dx              ; save registers
;
        mov     dl,al           ; in DL for DOS call
        mov     ah,2            ; standard output
        int     21h             ; DOS call
;
        pop     dx              ; restore registers
        ret                     ; return
stdout  endp
```

STDOUTDR

Direct Standard Output

Function: This routine sends individual characters out the standard output device using direct output.

Input: Upon entry an ASCII code is in AL.

Output: A single character is output through the direct standard output call.

Registers Used: AH is modified. AL is used for input.

Segments Referenced: None

Routines Called: DOS call number 6 (Direct console I/O) is used.

Special Notes: None

```
; ROUTINE FOR DIRECT CONSOLE OUTPUT
;
stdoutdr        proc    far
        push    dx              ; save registers
;
        cmp     al,ØFFh         ; check for the one case of input
        je      stdoutdrexit
        mov     dl,al           ; in DL for DOS call
        mov     ah,6            ; direct console output
        int     21h             ; DOS call
;
stdoutdrexit:
        pop     dx              ; restore registers
        ret                     ; return
stdoutdr        endp
```

STDCRLF

Standard Output of Carriage Return/Linefeed

Function: This routine sends a carriage return and then a linefeed out through the standard output device.

Input: None

Output: ASCII codes 13 for carriage return and the ASCII code 10 for linefeed are sent to the standard output device.

Registers Used: No registers are modified.

Segments Referenced: None

Routines Called: STDOUT

Special Notes: None

```
; ROUTINE TO SEND CR LF TO STANDARD OUTPUT
;
stdcrlf proc     far
        push     ax                ; save registers

        mov      al,13             ; ASCII carriage return
        call     stdout            ; send it out
        mov      al,1Ø             ; ASCII linefeed
        call     stdout            ; send it out

        pop      ax                ; restore registers
        ret                        ; return
stdcrlf endp
```

STDSPACE

Standard Output of Space

Function: This routine sends a space out through the standard output device.

Input: None

Output: ASCII code 32 for space is sent to the standard output device.

Registers Used: No registers are modified.

Segments Referenced: None

Routines Called: STDOUT

Special Notes: None

```
; ROUTINE TO SEND SPACE TO STANDARD OUTPUT
;
; A space is sent to the standard output device
;
stdspace        proc    far
        push    ax              ; save registers
;
        mov     al,32           ; ASCII space
        call    stdout          ; send it out
;
        pop     ax              ; restore registers
        ret                     ; return
stdspace        endp
```

STDMESSOUT

Standard Output of a Message

Function: This routine sends a message out through the standard output device.

Input: Upon input DS:SI points to the message. The message terminates with an ASCII zero.

Output: The individual characters of the message are output through the standard output device.

Registers Used: No registers are modified. SI is used to point to the input.

Segments Referenced: The data segment must contain the message.

Routines Called: STDOUT

Special Notes: None

```
; ROUTINE TO SEND MESSAGE TO STANDARD OUTPUT
;
stdmessout proc    far
        push    si              ; save registers
        push    ax
;
stdmessout1:
        mov     al,[si]         ; get byte
        inc     si              ; point to next byte
        cmp     al,Ø            ; done?
        je      stdmessoutexit  ; if so exit
        call    stdout          ; send it out
        jmp     stdmessout1     ; loop for more
;
stdmessoutexit:
        pop     ax              ; restore registers
        pop     si
        ret                     ; return
stdmessout      endp
```

COMINIT

Initialize Communications Line

Function: This routine initializes one of the two communications lines.

Input: Upon entry AL contains the initialization byte as follows:

7 6 5	4 3	2	1 0
—baud rate—	—parity—	—stop bit—	—word length—
000 = 110	00 = none	0 = 1	10 = 7 bits
001 = 150	01 = odd	1 = 2	11 = 8 bits
010 = 300	10 = none		
011 = 600	11 = even		
100 = 1200			
101 = 2400			
110 = 4800			
111 = 9600			

DX contains the unit number (0 for com1: and 1 for com2:).

Output: Output is sent to the hardware controlling the specified communications line.

Registers Used: No registers are modified.

Segments Referenced: None

Routines Called: BIOS interrupt 14h (RS-232 I/O) is used.

Special Notes: None

```
; ROUTINE TO INITIALIZE A COMMUNICATIONS LINE
;
cominit proc    far
;
        mov     ah,Ø            ; initialize
        int     14h             ; RS232 BIOS call
        ret                     ; return
;
cominit endp
```

COMINCK

Communications Line Input Check

Function: This routine checks, but does not wait for input from one of the two serial communications lines.

Input: Upon entry DX contains the unit number (0 for com1: and 1 for com2:). During the routine, input is from the specified communications line.

Output: If a byte is available, the routine returns with the flag condition NZ and the byte in AL, but if no byte is available then the routine returns with the flag condition Z, and AL is meaningless.

Registers Used: AH is modified. DX is used for input and AL is used for output.

Segments Referenced: During the routine the system data segment is referenced.

Routines Called: None

Special Notes: None

```
; ROUTINE TO CHECK FOR INPUT FROM A COMMUNICATIONS LINE
;
cominck proc     far
;
        push    ds              ; save registers
        push    dx
        push    si
;
        mov     si,dx           ; look up address of com line
        add     si,si           ; double to index into table
        mov     dx,40h          ; segment of table
        mov     ds,dx           ; set data segment to this table
        mov     dx,[si]         ; now get it
        add     dx,5            ; line status
        in      al,dx           ; get it
        test    al,1            ; receive buffer full?
        jz      cominckexit
```

```
;
        mov    dx, [si]         ; data register
        in     al, dx           ; get it
cominckexit:
;
        pop    si               ; restore registers
        pop    dx
        pop    ds
        ret
;
cominck endp
```

COMOUT

Communications Line Output

Function: This routine sends a byte out one of the two communications lines.

Input: Upon entry AL contains the byte to be sent out and DX contains the unit number (0 for com1: and 1 for com2:).

Output: Output is sent to the specified communications line.

Registers Used: No registers are modified.

Segments Referenced: None

Routines Called: BIOS interrupt 14h (RS-232 I/O) is used.

Special Notes: None

```
; ROUTINE TO SEND OUTPUT TO A COMMUNICATIONS LINE
;
comout  proc    far
;
        mov     ah,1            ; send it out
        int     14h             ; RS232 BIOS call
        ret                     ; return
comout  endp
```

COMON

Communications Line On

Function: This routine turns on the handshaking signals DTR (line 20) and RTS (line 4) on the specified communications line.

Input: Upon entry DX contains the unit number (0 for com1: and 1 for com2:).

Output: Just to the communications line.

Registers Used: No registers are modified. DX is used for input.

Segments Referenced: During the routine the system data segment is referenced.

Routines Called: None

Special Notes: None

```
; ROUTINE TO TURN ON INPUT FROM A COMMUNICATIONS LINE
;
comon   proc    far
;
        push    ds              ; save registers
        push    dx
        push    si
;
        mov     si,dx           ; look up address of com line
        add     si,si           ; double to index into table
        mov     dx,40h          ; segment of system I/O table
        mov     ds,dx           ; set data segment to this table
        mov     dx,[si]         ; now get it
        add     dx,4            ; modem control register
        mov     al,3            ; set DTR and RTS
        out     dx,al           ; send out control byte
;
        pop     si              ; restore registers
        pop     dx
        pop     ds
        ret
;
comon   endp
```

COMOFF

Communications Line Off

Function: This routine turns off the handshaking signal DTR (line 20) on the specified communications line. RTS (line 4) is kept as it was.

Input: Upon entry DX contains the unit number (0 for com1: and 1 for com2:).

Output: Just to the communications line.

Registers Used: No registers are modified. DX is used for input.

Segments Referenced: During the routine the system data segment is referenced.

Routines Called: None

Special Notes: None

```
; ROUTINE TO TURN OFF INPUT FROM A COMMUNICATIONS LINE

comoff  proc    far

        push    ds              ; save registers
        push    dx
        push    si

        mov     si,dx           ; look up address of com line
        add     si,si           ; double to index into table
        mov     dx,40h          ; segment of system I/O table
        mov     ds,dx           ; set data segment to this table
        mov     dx,[si]         ; now get it
        add     dx,4            ; modem control register
        mov     al,2            ; clear DTR (line 20)
        out     dx,al           ; send out control byte

        pop     si              ; restore registers
        pop     dx
        pop     ds
        ret
;
comoff  endp
```

Binary Conversions

*T*here are three basically different ways that numbers can be stored in a computer's memory. These are 1) binary integer, 2) binary coded decimal (BCD) integer, and 3) floating point. This chapter covers just the first type. The other two types each have a separate chapter devoted to them.

The routines in this chapter perform conversion between the IBM PC's 8- and 16-bit internal **binary** integer formats and all the popular external integer number bases: binary, octal, hexadecimal, and decimal. For each of these four number bases, there are three routines: one for input from external to 16-bit binary internal format; one for output from 8-bit binary internal format to the external representation; and one for output from 16-bit binary internal format to the external representation.

Little needs to be said about the significance and usefulness of these numerical conversion routines. Binary integers are the primary method used by the CPU to store numbers, and numbers stored in this format are used for a wide variety of purposes, including management of the operating system and its various utilities as well as basic general purpose integer computations. The vast internal use of these numbers is proportionately reflected in the number of times they need to be sent in or out of the computer, but they cannot be transmitted or handled on the outside without some kind of conversion. All four external representations are needed. Of the four types, decimal and hexadecimal are most popular, but binary and octal representations occur often enough that we have included them for completeness.

Each routine in this chapter is short and is based around a simple algorithm which has essentially one loop to handle the numbers digit by digit.

Throughout these routines we have used the 8088 registers in a very consistent manner. For example, AX is used for quick calculations or data movement; CL and CX are used for counting, multiplying, or dividing; and DL and DX are used to pass numerical data in and out of the routines.

BIN16IN

Conversion from ASCII Binary to Internal 16-Bit Binary

Function: This routine accepts a binary number from the standard input device and converts it to internal 16-bit binary form.

Input: The individual digits of the binary number are received in ASCII through a call to a standard I/O routine. The valid digits are 0 and 1. An ASCII code other than for a valid digit will terminate the routine.

Output: A 16-bit binary number is returned in the DX register.

Registers used: Only DX is modified. It returns the result.

Segments registered: None

Routines called: STDIN

Special notes: None

```
; ROUTINE TO CONVERT FROM ASCII BINARY TO INTERNAL 16-BIT BINARY
;
bin16in proc    far
;
        push    ax              ; save registers
;
        mov     dx,0            ;initialize DX as 0
;
bin16in1:
        call    stdin           ; digit comes in through AL
        sub     al,30h          ; subtract 30h
        jl      bin16in2        ; check if too low
        cmp     al,1
        jg      bin16in2        ; check if too high
        cbw                     ; convert to word
;
        sal     dx,1            ; shift DX left once
        add     dx,ax           ; add in digit
        jmp     bin16in1
;
bin16in2:
        pop     ax              ; restore registers
        ret                     ; return
;
bin16in endp
```

BIN8OUT

Conversion from 8-Bit Binary to ASCII Binary

Function: This routine accepts an 8-bit binary number in the DL register and converts it to ASCII binary form which is sent to the standard output device.

Input: Upon entry an 8-bit binary number is in the DL register.

Output: A string of ASCII digits representing a binary number is sent out through the standard output device.

Registers used: No registers are modified. DL is used for input.

Segments referenced: None

Routines called: STDOUT

Special notes: None

```
ROUTINE TO CONVERT FROM INTERNAL 8-BIT BINARY TO ASCII BINARY

n8out proc     far

a binary number is in DL

        push    cx              ; save registers
        push    ax

        mov     cx,8            ;loop for a count of 8
n8out1:
        rol     dl,1            ; rotate DL left once
        mov     al,dl           ; move into AL
        and     al,1            ; just keep digit
        add     al,30h          ; add 30h to AL
        call    stdout          ; send it out
        loop    bin8out1

        pop     ax              ; restore registers
        pop     cx
        ret                     ;return

n8out endp
```

BIN16OUT

Conversion from 16-Bit Binary to ASCII Binary

Function: This routine accepts a 16-bit binary number in the DX register and converts it to ASCII binary form which is sent to the standard output device.

Input: Upon entry a 16-bit binary number is in the DX register.

Output: A string of ASCII digits representing a binary number is sent out through the standard output device.

Registers used: No registers are modified. DX is used for input.

Segments referenced: None

Routines called: STDOUT

Special notes: None

```
; ROUTINE TO CONVERT FROM INTERNAL 16-BIT BINARY TO ASCII BINARY
;
bin16out        proc    far
;
; a binary number is in DX
;
        push    cx              ; save registers
        push    ax
;
        mov     cx,16           ; loop for a count of 16
bin16out1:
        rol     dx,1            ; rotate DX left once
        mov     al,dl           ; move into AL
        and     al,1            ; just keep digit
        add     al,30h          ; add 30h to AL
        call    stdout          ; send it out
        loop    bin16out1
;
        pop     ax              ; restore registers
        pop     cx
        ret                     ; return
;
bin16out        endp
```

OCT16IN

Conversion from ASCII Octal to 16-Bit Binary

Function: This routine accepts an octal number from the standard input device and converts it to internal 16-bit binary form.

Input: The individual digits of the octal number are received in ASCII through a call to a standard I/O routine. The valid digits are 0 through 7. An ASCII code other than for a valid digit will terminate the routine.

Output: A 16-bit binary number is returned in the DX register.

Registers used: Only DX is modified. It returns the result.

Segments referenced: None

Routines called: STDIN

Special notes: None

```
ROUTINE TO CONVERT FROM ASCII OCTAL TO INTERNAL 16-BIT BINARY

oct16in proc    far

        push    cx              ; save registers
        push    ax

        mov     dx,0            ; initialize DX as 0

oct16in1:
        call    stdin           ; a digit comes in AL
        sub     al,30h          ; subtract 30h
        jl      oct16in2        ; check if too low
        cmp     al,7
        jg      oct16in2        ; check if too high
        cbw                     ; convert to word

        mov     cl,3
        sal     dx,cl           ; shift DX left once
        add     dx,ax           ; add in digit
        jmp     oct16in1
```

```
;
oct16in2:
        pop     ax              ; restore registers
        pop     cx
        ret                     ; return
;
oct16in endp
```

OCT8OUT

Conversion from 8-Bit Binary to ASCII Octal

Function: This routine accepts an 8-bit binary number in the DL register and converts it to ASCII octal form which is sent to the standard output device.

Input: Upon entry an 8-bit binary number is in the DL register.

Output: A string of ASCII digits representing an octal number is sent out through the standard output device.

Registers used: No registers are modified. DL is used for input.

Segments referenced: None

Routines called: STDOUT

Special notes: None

```
ROUTINE TO CONVERT FROM INTERNAL 8-BIT BINARY TO ASCII OCTAL

t8out proc     far

a binary number is in DL

        push    cx              ; save registers
        push    ax

first octal digit has only 2 bits
        mov     cl,2            ; for a count of 2
        rol     dl,cl           ;  rotate DL left

        mov     al,dl           ; move into AL
        and     al,3            ; just keep digit
        add     al,30h          ; add 30h to AL
        call    stdout          ; send it out

second and third octal digits have 3 bits each
        mov     cx,2            ;loop for a count of 2
t8out1:
        push    cx              ; save the count   .
        mov     cl,3            ; for a count of 3
        rol     dl,cl           ;  rotate DL left
```

```
;
        mov     al,dl           ; move into AL
        and     al,7            ; just keep digit
        add     al,30h          ; add 30h to AL
        call    stdout          ; send it out
        pop     cx              ; restore count
        loop    oct8out1
;
        pop     ax              ; restore registers
        pop     cx
        ret                     ; return
;
oct8out endp
```

OCT16OUT

Conversion from 16-bit Binary to ASCII Octal

Function: This routine accepts a 16-bit binary number in the DX register and converts it to ASCII octal form which is sent to the standard output device.

Input: Upon entry a 16-bit binary number is in the DX register.

Output: A string of ASCII digits representing an octal number is sent out through the standard output device.

Registers used: No registers are modified. DX is used for input.

Segments referenced: None

Routines called: STDOUT

Special notes: None

```
ROUTINE TO CONVERT FROM INTERNAL 16-BIT BINARY TO ASCII OCTAL

t16out          proc    far

a binary number is in DX

        push    cx              ; save registers
        push    ax

first octal digit has only one bit
        rol     dx,1            ; rotate DX left once

        mov     al,dl           ; move into AL
        and     al,1            ; just keep digit
        add     al,30h          ; add 30h to AL
        call    stdout          ; send it out

last five octal digits have 3 bits each
        mov     cx,5            ;loop for a count of 5
ct16out1:
        push    cx              ; save the count
        mov     cl,3            ; for a count of 3
        rol     dx,cl           ;  rotate DL left
```

```
;
        mov     al,dl           ; move into AL
        and     al,7            ; just keep digit
        add     al,30h          ; add 30h to AL
        call    stdout          ; send it out
        pop     cx              ; restore count
        loop    oct16out1
;
        pop     ax              ; restore registers
        pop     cx
        ret                     ;return
;
oct16out        endp
```

HEX16IN

Conversion from ASCII Hexadecimal to 16-Bit Binary

Function: This routine accepts a hexadecimal number from the standard input device and converts it to internal 16-bit binary form.

Input: The individual digits of the hexadecimal number are received in ASCII through a call to a standard I/O routine. The valid digits are 0 through 9 and A through F. An ASCII code other than for a valid digit will terminate the routine.

Output: A 16-bit binary number is returned in the DX register.

Registers used: Only DX is modified. It returns the result.

Segments referenced: None

Routines called: STDIN

Special notes: None

```
ROUTINE TO CONVERT FROM ASCII HEXADECIMAL TO INTERNAL 16-BIT BINARY

ex16in proc    far

       push    cx              ; save registers
       push    ax

       mov     dx,Ø            ; initialize DX as Ø

ex16in1:
       call    stdin           ; a digit comes in AL
       sub     al,3Øh          ; subtract 3Øh
       jl      hex16in3        ; check if too low
       cmp     al,9
       jle     hex16in2        ; go if ok
       and     al,5Fh          ; for lower case too
       sub     al,7            ; adjust for A-F
       jl      hex16in3        ; too low for A-F
       cmp     al,15           ; check if too high
       jg      hex16in3
```

```
;
hex16in2:
        cbw
        mov     cl,4            ; for a count of 4
        sal     dx,cl           ;  shift DX left
        add     dx,ax           ; add in digit
        jmp     hex16in1
;
hex16in3:
        pop     ax              ; restore registers
        pop     cx
        ret                     ; return
;
hex16in endp
```

HEX8OUT

Conversion from 8-Bit Binary to ASCII Hexadecimal

Function: This routine accepts an 8-bit binary number in the DL register and converts it to ASCII hexadecimal form which is sent to the standard output device.

Input: Upon entry an 8-bit binary number is in the DL register.

Output: A string of ASCII digits representing a hexadecimal number is sent out through the standard output device.

Registers used: No registers are modified. DL is used for input.

Segments referenced: None

Routines called: STDOUT

Special notes: None

```
ROUTINE TO CONVERT FROM INTERNAL 8-BIT BINARY TO ASCII HEXADECIMAL

ex8out proc     far

a binary number is in DL

        push    cx              ; save registers
        push    ax

        mov     cx,2            ; loop for a count of 2
ex8out1:
        push    cx              ; save the count
        mov     cl,4            ; for a count of 4
        rol     dl,cl           ;  rotate DL left

        mov     al,dl           ; move into AL
        and     al,ØØFh         ; just digit
        daa                     ; add 6 if A-F
        add     al,ØFØh         ; bump a carry if A-F
        adc     al,Ø4Øh         ; here is the ASCII
        call    stdout          ; send it out
```

```
;
        pop     cx
        loop    hex8out1
;
        pop     ax              ; restore registers
        pop     cx
        ret                     ; return
;
hex8out endp
```

HEX16OUT

Conversion from 16-Bit binary to ASCII Hexadecimal

Function: This routine accepts a 16-bit binary number in the DX register and converts it to ASCII hexadecimal form which is sent to the standard output device.

Input: Upon entry a 16-bit binary number is in the DX register.

Output: A string of ASCII digits representing a hexadecimal number is sent out through the standard output device.

Registers used: No registers are modified. DX is used for input.

Segments referenced: None

Routines called: STDOUT

Special notes: None

```
ROUTINE TO CONVERT FROM INTERNAL 16-BIT BINARY TO ASCII HEXADECIMAL

hex16out        proc    far

a binary number is in DX

        push    cx              ; save registers
        push    ax

        mov     cx,4            ; loop for a count of 4
hex16out1:
        push    cx              ; save the count
        mov     cl,4            ; for a count of 4
        rol     dx,cl           ;  rotate DX left

        mov     al,dl           ; move into AL
        and     al,00Fh         ; just the digit
        daa                     ; add 6 if A-F
        add     al,0F0h         ; bump a carry if A-F
        adc     al,040h         ; here is the ASCII
        call    stdout          ; send it out
```

```
;
        pop     cx
        loop    hex16out1
;
        pop     ax              ; restore registers
        pop     cx
        ret                     ; return
;
hex16out        endp
```

DEC16IN

Conversion from ASCII Decimal to 16-Bit Binary

Function: This routine accepts a decimal number from the standard input device and converts it to internal 16-bit binary form.

Input: The individual digits of the decimal number are received in ASCII through a call to a standard I/O routine. The valid digits are 0 through 9. An ASCII code other than for a valid digit will terminate the routine.

Output: A 16-bit binary number is returned in the DX register.

Registers used: Only DX is modified. It returns the result.

Segments referenced: None

Routines called: STDIN

Special notes: None

```
; ROUTINE TO CONVERT FROM ASCII DECIMAL TO INTERNAL 16-BIT BINARY
;
;
dec16in proc    far
;
        push    cx              ; save registers
        push    ax

        mov     dx,Ø            ; initialize DX as Ø
;
dec16in1:
        call    stdin           ; digit comes in AL
        sub     al,30h          ; subtract 30h
        jl      dec16in2        ; check if too low
        cmp     al,9
        jg      dec16in2        ; check if too high
        cbw                     ; convert to word
;
        push    ax              ; save digit
        mov     ax,dx
        mov     cx,1Ø           ; multiplier of 1Ø
        mul     cx              ; multiply
        mov     dx,ax           ; result in DX
        pop     ax              ; restore digit
```

```
        add     dx,ax           ; add in digit
        jmp     dec16in1
;
dec16in2:
        pop     ax              ; restore registers
        pop     cx
        ret                     ; return
;
dec16in endp
```

DEC8OUT

Conversion from 8-Bit Binary to ASCII Decimal

Function: This routine accepts an 8-bit binary number in the DL register and converts it to ASCII decimal form which is sent to the standard output device.

Input: Upon entry an 8-bit binary number is in the DL register.

Output: A string of ASCII digits representing a decimal number is stored in a buffer called TBUFF and then sent out through the standard output device.

Registers used: No registers are modified. DL is used for input.

Segments referenced: DATAS is a data segment which contains TBUFF.

Routines called: STDOUT

Special notes: None

```
; ROUTINE TO CONVERT FROM INTERNAL 8-BIT BINARY TO ASCII DECIMAL

dec8out proc    far

        push    ds              ; save registers
        push    di
        push    dx
        push    cx
        push    ax

        mov     ax,datas        ; point to the data segment
        mov     ds,ax

; a binary number is in DL
;
; put the digits in a buffer
;
        mov     cx,Ø            ; initialize a counter
        mov     di,offset tbuff ; point to buffer
dec8out1:
        push    cx              ; save CX
        mov     al,dl           ; AX has numerator
        mov     ah,Ø            ; clear upper half
```

```
              mov     cl,1Ø           ; divisor of 1Ø
              div     cl              ; divide
              mov     dl,al           ; get quotient
              mov     al,ah           ; get remainder
;
              add     al,3Øh          ; add 3Øh
              mov     [di],al         ; put in buffer
              inc     di              ; point to next byte
;
              pop     cx              ; restore CX
              inc     cx              ; count the digit
              cmp     dl,Ø            ; done?
              jnz     dec8out1
;
; dump the buffer out
;
dec8out2:
              dec     di              ; back up through the buffer
              mov     al,[di]         ; get the byte from the buffer
              call    stdout          ; send it out
              loop    dec8out2
;
              pop     ax              ; restore registers
              pop     cx
              pop     dx
              pop     di
              pop     ds
              ret                     ; return
;
dec8out endp
```

DEC16OUT

Conversion from 16-Bit Binary to ASCII Decimal

Function: This routine accepts a 16-bit binary number in the DX register and converts it to ASCII decimal form which is sent to the standard output device.

Input: Upon entry a 16-bit binary number is in the DX register.

Output: A string of ASCII digits representing a decimal number is stored in a buffer called TBUFF and then sent out through the standard output device.

Registers used: No registers are modified. DX is used for input.

Segments referenced: DATAS is a data segment which contains TBUFF.

Routines called: STDOUT

Special notes: None

```
; ROUTINE TO CONVERT FROM INTERNAL 16-BIT BINARY TO ASCII DECIMAL
;
;
dec16out        proc    far
;
        push    ds              ; save registers
        push    di
        push    dx
        push    cx
        push    ax
;
        mov     ax,datas        ; point to data segment
        mov     ds,ax
;
;number is in DX
;
; put the digits in a buffer
;
        mov     cx,Ø            ; initialize the counter
        lea     di, tbuff       ; point to the buffer
dec16out1:
        push    cx              ; save CX
        mov     ax,dx           ; numerator
        mov     dx,Ø            ; clear upper half
```

```
        mov     cx,1Ø           ; divisor of 1Ø
        div     cx              ; divide
        xchg    ax,dx           ; get quotient
;
        add     al,3Øh          ; add 3Øh
        mov     [di],al         ; put in buffer
        inc     di              ; next byte
;
        pop     cx              ; restore CX for the count
        inc     cx              ; count the digit
        cmp     dx,Ø            ; done?
        jnz     dec16out1
;
; dump the buffer out
;
dec16out2:
        dec     di              ; back up through the buffer
        mov     al,[di]         ; get byte from buffer
        call    stdout          ; send it out
        loop    dec16out2
;
        pop     ax              ; restore registers
        pop     cx
        pop     dx
        pop     di
        pop     ds
        ret                     ; return
;
dec16out        endp
```

BCD Conversions

*T*his chapter contains routines which convert between internal binary coded decimal (BCD) and other formats, both internal and external. Here are routines to convert between external decimal representation and internal BCD representation and between internal binary and internal BCD.

The internal BCD format packs two decimal digits per byte, one per nibble. By using a large number of bytes, you can precisely represent high precision decimal numbers. These routines use 18 bytes of storage to handle 36-digit BCD numbers, but can easily be modified to handle other sizes.

Fixed point numbers can be handled by assigning a fixed position for a decimal point. For example, dollars and cents can be handled by assigning the decimal point so that there are exactly two BCD digits to its right which form the fractional part of the number.

BCD notation is important in applications such as finance and accounting which deal with high precision integers and fixed point numbers. The fact that they can precisely represent fixed point decimal numbers is extremely important to these applications.

These routines use the same basic looping algorithm as those in the previous chapter. However, there is now an additional complication of packing and unpacking digits into the BCD bytes of memory.

BCDIN

Conversion from ASCII Decimal to BCD

Function: This routine accepts a decimal number from the standard input device and converts it to internal BCD format.

Input: The individual digits of the decimal number are received in ASCII through a call to a standard I/O routine. The valid digits are 0 through 9. An ASCII code other than for a valid digit will terminate the routine.

Output: On return a 36-digit number is stored in BCD form in an 18-byte buffer called BCDBUFF.

Registers used: No registers are modified.

Segments referenced: DATAS is a data segment which contains BCDBUFF.

Routines called: STDIN

Special notes: None

```
; ROUTINE TO CONVERT FROM ASCII DECIMAL TO INTERNAL BCD FORMAT
;
bcdin   proc    far
;
        push    ds              ; save registers
        push    di
        push    dx
        push    cx
        push    ax
;
; set up data segment
        mov     ax,datas        ; point to data segment
        mov     ds,ax
;
; clear bcd buffer
        lea     di,bcdbuff      ; point to BCD buffer
        mov     al,Ø            ; zero byte
        mov     cx,18           ; buffer size
bcdin1:
        mov     [di],al         ; zero the byte
        inc     di              ; point to next byte
        loop    bcdin1
```

bcdin2:
; get the digit
```
        call    stdin           ; digit comes in AL
        sub     al,3Øh          ; subtract 3Øh
        jl      bcdin4          ; check if too low
        cmp     al,9
        jg      bcdin4          ; check if too high
```

; multiply buffer by 1Ø and add new digit
```
        lea     di,bcdbuff      ; point to bcd buffer
        mov     cx,18           ; buffer size
```
bcdin3:
```
        push    cx              ; save counter
        mov     dl,al           ; save previous digit
        mov     al,[di]         ; pick up byte from buffer
        mov     cl,4            ; for a count of 4
        sal     ax,cl           ;  shift byte left
        or      al,dl           ; combine with previous digit
        mov     [di],al         ; result goes back
        mov     al,ah           ; prepare for next byte
        and     al,ØFh          ; strip to byte
        inc     di              ; point to next byte
        pop     cx              ; restore count

        loop    bcdin3

        jmp     bcdin2
```

bcdin4:
```
        pop     ax              ; restore registers
        pop     cx
        pop     dx
        pop     di
        pop     ds
        ret                     ; return
```

bcdin   endp

BCDOUT

Conversion from BCD to ASCII Decimal

Function: This routine converts a 36-digit number stored in BCD form to ASCII decimal form which is sent to the standard output device.

Input: Upon entry a 36-digit number is stored in an 18-byte BCD buffer called BCDBUFF.

Output: A string of ASCII digits representing a decimal number is stored in a buffer called TBUFF and then sent out through a standard I/O routine.

Registers used: No registers are modified.

Segments referenced: DATAS is a data segment containing BCDBUFF and TBUFF.

Routines called: STDOUT

Special notes: None

```
; ROUTINE TO CONVERT FROM INTERNAL BCD TO ASCII DECIMAL
;
bcdout  proc    far
;
        push    ds              ; save registers
        push    si
        push    dx
        push    cx
        push    ax
;
; set up data segment
        mov     ax,datas        ; point to data segment
        mov     ds,ax
;
        mov     cx,18           ; for a count of 18
        lea     si,bcdbuff      ; point to bcd buffer
        add     si,17           ; point to end of bcd buffer
        mov     dh,Ø            ; clear flag for leading zeros
```

```
bcdout1:
        push    cx              ; save loop count
        mov     al,[si]         ; get BCD byte
        dec     si              ; and point to next
        mov     dl,al           ; save it

    upper digit
        mov     cl,4            ; for a count of 4
        rol     al,cl           ;   rotate byte
        and     al,ØFh          ; just the digit
        or      dh,al           ; leading zeros?
        jz      bcdout2         ; if so skip digit
        add     al,3Øh          ; make ASCII
        call    stdout          ; send it out
bcdout2:

        pop     cx              ; restore count
        cmp     cx,1            ; last digit?
        jnz     bcdout3         ; skip if not
        mov     dh,ØFFh         ;   set flag if so
bcdout3:
        push    cx              ; save count

        mov     al,dl           ; byte back

    lower digit
        and     al,ØFh          ; just the digit
        or      dh,al           ; leading zeros?
        jz      bcdout4         ; if so skip digit
        add     al,3Øh          ; make ASCII
        call    stdout          ; send it out
bcdout4:

        pop     cx              ; restore loop count
        loop    bcdout1

        pop     ax              ; restore registers
        pop     cx
        pop     dx
        pop     si
        pop     ds
        ret                     ; return

bcdout  endp
```

BCD2I16

Conversion from BCD to 16-Bit Binary

Function: This routine converts from internal BCD format to internal binary format.

Input: Upon entry a 36-digit number is contained in an 18-digit BCD buffer called BCDBUFF.

Output: A 16-bit binary number is returned in the DX register.

Registers used: Only DX is modified. DX is used for output.

Segments referenced: DATAS is a data segment which contains the buffer BCDBUFF.

Routines called: None

Special notes: None

```
; ROUTINE TO CONVERT FROM INTERNAL BCD TO INTERNAL 16-BIT BINARY
;
bcd2i16 proc    far
;
        push    ds              ; save registers
        push    si
        push    cx
        push    ax
;
; set up data segment
        mov     ax,datas        ; point to data segment
        mov     ds,ax
;
; set up loop
        mov     cx,18           ; initialize counter
        lea     si,bcdbuff      ; point to buffer
        add     si,17           ; point to end of bcd buffer
        mov     dx,Ø            ; set DX to zero
;
bcd2i161:
        push    cx              ; save loop count
        mov     al,[si]         ; get BCD byte
        dec     si              ; and point to next
        mov     bl,al           ; save it
```

```
;
; upper digit
        mov     cl,4            ; for a count of 4
        rol     al,cl           ;  rotate byte
        and     al,ØFh          ; just the digit
        cbw
;
        push    ax              ; save digit
        mov     ax,dx
        mov     cx,1Ø           ; multiplier of 1Ø
        mul     cx              ; multiply
        mov     dx,ax           ; result in DX
        pop     ax              ; restore digit
;
        add     dx,ax           ; add in digit
;
        mov     al,bl           ; byte back
;
; lower digit
        and     al,ØFh          ; just the digit
        cbw
;
        push    ax              ; save digit
        mov     ax,dx
        mov     cx,1Ø           ; multiplier of 1Ø
        mul     cx              ; multiply
        mov     dx,ax           ; result in DX
        pop     ax              ; restore digit
;
        add     dx,ax           ; add in digit
;
        pop     cx              ; restore loop count
        loop    bcd2i161
;
        pop     ax              ; restore registers
        pop     cx
        pop     si
        pop     ds
        ret                     ; return
;
bcd2i16 endp
```

I162BCD

Conversion from 16-Bit Binary to BCD

Function: This routine converts internal 16-bit binary numbers to numbers stored in internal BCD format.

Input: Upon entry a 16-bit binary number is in the DX register.

Output: On return a 36-digit number is stored in BCD form in an 18-byte buffer called BCDBUFF.

Registers used: No registers are modified. DX is used for input.

Segments referenced: DATAS is a data segment containing BCDBUFF.

Routines called: None

Special notes: None

```
; ROUTINE TO CONVERT FROM INTERNAL 16-BIT BINARY TO INTERNAL BCD
;
i162bcd proc    far
;
        push    ds              ; save registers
        push    di
        push    dx
        push    cx
        push    ax
;
; set up data segment
        mov     ax,datas        ; point to data segment
        mov     ds,ax
;
; a binary number is in DX
;
; clear bcd buffer
        lea     di,bcdbuff      ; point to buffer
        mov     al,Ø            ; zero byte
        mov     cx,18           ; buffer size
i162bcd1:
        mov     [di],al         ; clear byte
        inc     di              ; next byte
        loop    i162bcd1
```

```
; put the digits in a buffer
        lea     di,bcdbuff      ; point to buffer
i62bcd2:
        mov     ax,dx           ; numerator
        mov     dx,Ø            ; clear upper half
        mov     cx,1Ø           ; divisor of 1Ø
        div     cx              ; divide
        xchg    ax,dx           ; get quotient
        mov     bl,al           ; save digit

        mov     ax,dx           ; numerator
        mov     dx,Ø            ; clear upper half
        mov     cx,1Ø           ; divisor of 1Ø
        div     cx              ; divide
        xchg    ax,dx           ; get quotient

        mov     cl,4            ; for a count of 4
        rol     al,cl           ;  rotate digit
        and     al,ØFØh         ; just the digit
        or      al,bl           ; combine digits

        mov     [di],al         ; put in buffer
        inc     di              ; next byte
        cmp     dx,Ø            ; done?
        jnz     i162bcd2

        pop     ax              ; restore registers
        pop     cx
        pop     dx
        pop     di
        pop     ds
        ret                     ; return

i62bcd endp
```

Floating Point Conversion

Programs

Floating Point Input

SGNDEC16IN	Conversion from ASCII Signed Decimal to Binary
TFP2SFP	Conversion from Temporary to Single Precision
FPINDIGIT	Single Decimal Digit to Floating Point
FPTNORM	Normalization of Temporary Floating Point
FPTMUL	Multiplication of Temporary Floating Point by 10
FPTDIV	Division of Temporary Floating Point Number by 10
FPIN	Conversion from External to Internal Floating Point

Floating Point Output

SFP2TFP	Conversion from Single Precision to Temporary Floating Point
TDECSHOW	Display of Floating Point
BIN802DEC	Conversion from 80-Bit Binary to Decimal Digits
DECNORM	Normalization of Temporary Decimal Floating Point
DECHALF	Halving a Temporary Decimal Floating Point Number
DECDOUBLE	Doubling a Temporary Decimal Floating Point Number
FPOUT	Conversion from Internal to External Floating Point

Internal Floating Point Conversions	
FIX	Conversion from Floating Point to 16-Bit Integer
FLOAT	Conversion from 16-Bit Integer to Floating Point
SFP2DFP	Conversion from Single to Double Precision Floating
DFP2SFP	Conversion from Double to Single Precision Floating

*T*his chapter contains routines which perform conversions involving floating point representations of numbers.

Floating point representation is important because it provides a way to represent real numbers, which are the fundamental type of number used in scientific calculations. Actually, floating point representation cannot accurately represent every real number because that would require infinite precision. Instead, it uses the separate components of numbers (sign, exponent, and mantissa) to achieve a wide range of magnitudes with good precision in both negative and positive values.

There are three major sections: one for floating point input, one for floating point output, and one for internal floating point conversions. The algorithms for floating point number conversions are much more complex than for integers. Here we must deal with exponents, signs, and normalization. The conversion routines for floating point numbers require several support routines (given first), each about as complex as just one of the integer conversion routines of the previous two chapters.

Use of Equates for Addressing

Throughout the routines that follow equates have been used to shorten the address fields. This keeps the comment fields of uniform width throughout the code, leaving plenty of room for comments on every line of code. For example, instead of writing:

```
ar      word ptr [di+8],1        ; shift right all bytes
```

which causes the comment field to start way over in column 41, we write:

```
sar     diword+8,1      ; shift right all bytes
```

in which the comment field starts in the usual column 33. The following equate would appear near the beginning of the assembly-language module:

```
diword equ     word ptr [di]
```

All equates can be placed in one section at the beginning of your assembly module and can be used in any of the programs within that module. Below is a complete list of equates used for addressing in this chapter.

```
sibyte          equ     byte ptr [si]
siword          equ     word ptr [si]
dibyte          equ     byte ptr [di]
diword          equ     word ptr [di]

sfpbuffwØ       equ     word ptr sfpbuff+Ø
sfpbuffb2       equ     byte ptr sfpbuff+2
sfpbuffb3       equ     byte ptr sfpbuff+3
sfpbuffw2       equ     word ptr sfpbuff+2

dfpbuffwØ       equ     word ptr dfpbuff+Ø
dfpbuffw2       equ     word ptr dfpbuff+2
dfpbuffw4       equ     word ptr dfpbuff+4
dfpbuffw6       equ     word ptr dfpbuff+6

fptemp1wØ       equ     word ptr fptemp1+Ø
fptemp1w2       equ     word ptr fptemp1+2
fptemp1w4       equ     word ptr fptemp1+4
fptemp1w6       equ     word ptr fptemp1+6
fptemp1w8       equ     word ptr fptemp1+8
fptemp1b1Ø      equ     byte ptr fptemp1+1Ø
fptemp1w11      equ     word ptr fptemp1+11

fptemp2wØ       equ     word ptr fptemp2+Ø
fptemp2w2       equ     word ptr fptemp2+2
fptemp2w4       equ     word ptr fptemp2+4
fptemp2w6       equ     word ptr fptemp2+6
fptemp2w8       equ     word ptr fptemp2+8
fptemp2b1Ø      equ     byte ptr fptemp2+1Ø
fptemp2w11      equ     word ptr fptemp2+11
```

Floating Point Formats

We will use four different internal floating point representations. The first two are standard binary formats used by the BASICs for the IBM PC, and the last two are temporary formats which are designed to make the conversion calculations easier. The idea of temporary floating point formats is not new. For example, the Intel 8087 numeric processor chip which can be used in the IBM PC also uses a temporary format for internal processing.

The main difference between standard formats and temporary formats is that the various components are tightly packed in standard formats whereas they are loosely packed in temporary formats. The tight packing of standard formats makes it difficult to access the individual components, and so the loose packing of temporary formats increases the efficiency of computations. In temporary formats the exponents are stored in the more common and easier-to-work-with two's complement binary format, again increasing the efficiency of computations.

Another difference between standard and temporary formats is that temporary formats have more precision in their mantissas and exponents

Name	Exponent format	Exponent base	Sign	Mantissa	Total storage
Single precision binary	8 bits binary biased by 128	Two	1 bit	24 bits binary	4 bytes
Double precision binary	8 bits binary biased by 128	Two	1 bit	40 bits binary	8 bytes
Temporary binary	16 bits 2's complement binary	Two	1 byte	72 bits binary +8 extra	13 bytes
Temporary decimal	16 bits 2's complement binary	Ten	1 byte	25 decimal digits	28 bytes

Table 5-1.   Internal floating point representations

than standard internal or external formats. This allows room for round-off errors which accumulate during the conversion process. Our temporary formats give more than enough leeway for this.

Table 5-1 shows vital statistics of the four internal floating point formats we have used. Figure 5-1 displays these formats pictorially.

One of the temporary formats is binary and the other is decimal. The temporary binary format is used with floating point input and the temporary decimal format is used with floating point output.

In addition to these internal formats, there is an external floating point format. It has a decimal mantissa and decimal exponent and corresponds closely to the usual scientific notation. In more detail, it consists of a sign character which is blank or minus, followed by decimal digits of the mantissa with one embedded decimal point to the right of the first significant digit. Following the mantissa is an exponent which

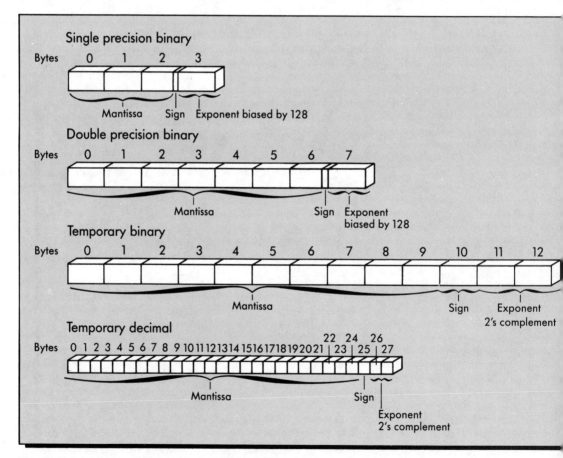

Figure 5-1. Internal floating point representations

starts with the letter E, then a sign, then a decimal number. For example, −123.431 is represented by:

```
.23431E+2
```

loating Point Input

The main routine of this section converts from external decimal floating point to internal single precision binary floating point formats discussed above.

Preceding the main routine are a number of support routines. These include routines designed for conversion from temporary binary floating point to single precision; conversion from digit to floating point; multiplication and division by 10; and normalization. Multiplication and division by 10 are key steps in the conversion algorithm that is a generalization of the basic algorithm used for integer conversions.

The support routines are "near" procedures. That is, they cannot be called from outside their own segment. Though they perform reasonably general actions, they are designed to work under the special conditions which occur within this particular conversion algorithm. For example, not all registers are preserved and normalization assumes that the mantissa is too large, not allowing for the case in which it might be too small. Even so, we have given these routines regular headers to better explain their function.

SGNDEC16IN

Conversion from ASCII Signed Decimal to Binary

Function: This routine accepts a signed decimal number from the standard input device and converts it to internal signed two's complement 16-bit binary form.

Input: Individual digits of the signed decimal number are received in ASCII through a call to a standard input routine. The sign ($\pm$) is optional and the valid digits are 0 through 9. An ASCII code other than that for the sign and the valid digits will terminate the routine.

Output: A signed two's complement 16-bit binary number is returned in the DX register.

Registers used: AX and CX are modified. DX is used for output.

Segments referenced: None

Routines called: STDIN

Special notes: None

```
; ROUTINE TO CONVERT FROM ASCII SIGNED DECIMAL TO INTERNAL TWO'S
; COMPLEMENT 16-BIT BINARY
;
sgndec16in      proc      far
;
        mov     dx,Ø            ; initialize DX as Ø
        mov     ch,Ø            ; sign flag
;
        call    stdin           ; look for sign
        cmp     al,'-'          ; minus
        jz      sgndec16in1     ; store it
        cmp     al,'+'          ; plus
        jz      sgndec16in2     ; ignore it
        jmp     sgndec16in3     ; anything else gets used
;
sgndec16in1:
; set sign as negative
        mov     ch,ØFFh         ; ØFFh is -1
;
```

```
sgndec16in2:
; normal loop
        call    stdin           ; digit comes in AL

sgndec16in3:
; already have a digit?
        sub     al,30h          ; subtract 30h
        jl      sgndec16in4     ; check if too low
        cmp     al,9
        jg      sgndec16in4     ; check if too high
        cbw                     ; convert to word

        push    cx              ; save sign
        push    ax              ; save digit
        mov     ax,dx
        mov     cx,10           ; multiplier of ten
        mul     cx              ; multiply
        mov     dx,ax           ; result in DX
        pop     ax              ; restore digit

        add     dx,ax           ; add in digit
        pop     cx              ; restore count
        jmp     sgndec16in2

sgndec16in4:
; resolve the sign
        cmp     ch,0            ; is it there?
        je      sgndec16in5     ; if not skip

        neg     dx              ; was a negative

sgndec16in5:
        ret                     ; return

sgndec16in   endp
```

TFP2SFP

Conversion from Temporary to Single Precision

Function: This routine converts from temporary binary floating point to single precision floating point.

Input: Upon entry a number is stored in temporary binary floating point form in FPTEMP1. The temporary binary floating point number has a 72-bit binary mantissa with 8 bits to the left of these for internal use, a sign byte, and a 16-bit two's complement binary exponent (see Figure 5-2).

Output: Upon exit a single precision floating point number is stored in SFPBUFF. The single precision floating point number has a 24-bit binary mantissa, a sign bit, and an 8-bit exponent biased by 128 (see Figure 5-3).

Registers used: AX and DX are modified.

Segments referenced: Upon entry the data segment contains the messages INTERNAL, UNDERFLOW, and OVERFLOW, and storage for the temporary binary floating point number FPTEMP1 and the single precision floating point number SFPBUFF.

Routines called: STDSPACE, MESSOUT, and HEX16OUT.

Special notes: Equates are used to shorten address fields. This is a near procedure needed by FPIN.

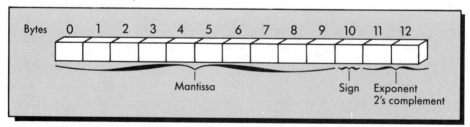

Figure 5-2.   Temporary binary floating point

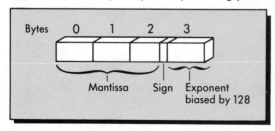

Figure 5-3.   Single precision binary floating point

ROUTINE TO CONVERT FROM TEMP FLOATING POINT TO SINGLE PRECISION
FLOATING POINT

```
tp2sfp proc     near

move mantissa
        mov     ax,fptemp1w4    ; below word
        rcl     ax,1            ; carry for round up
        mov     ax,fptemp1w6    ; low word
        adc     ax,Ø            ; low word + carry
        mov     sfpbuffwØ,ax    ; put in place
        mov     dx,ax           ; check for zero

        mov     ax,fptemp1w8
        or      dx,ax           ; check this part too
        and     ax,ØØ7Fh        ; just bottom 7 bits
        mov     sfpbuffw2,ax    ; put in place

move sign bit
        mov     al,fptemp1b1Ø   ; byte 1Ø is sign
        and     al,80h
        or      sfpbuffb2,al    ; bit 7 is sign

move exponent
        mov     ax,fptemp1w11   ; 16-bit 2's complement exponent
        cmp     ax,-128         ; too low?
        jl      tfp2sfp2        ; error message
        cmp     ax,127          ; too high?
        jg      tfp2sfp3        ; error message

        add     ax,80h          ; bias
        cmp     dx,Ø            ; was mantissa Ø?
        jne     tfp2sfp1
        mov     al,Ø            ; then -128 exponent
tfp2sfp1:
        mov     sfpbuffb3,al    ; put biased byte back

normal return

show hex for debugging
        lea     si,internal     ; point to message
        call    stdmessout      ; send message

        mov     dx,sfpbuffw2    ; upper word
        call    hex16out        ; show it

        mov     dx,sfpbuffwØ    ; lower word
        call    hex16out        ; show it
```

```
;
        call    stdspace        ; skip space
        clc                     ; clear carry
        ret                     ; return
;
; underflow error
tfp2sfp2:
        lea     si,underflow    ; point to message
        jmp     tfp2sfp4
;
; overflow error
tfp2sfp3:
        lea     si,overflow     ; point to message
        jmp     tfp2sfp4
;
tfp2sfp4:
        call    stdmessout      ; send message
        stc                     ; set carry
        ret                     ; return
;
tfp2sfp endp
```

FPINDIGIT

Single Decimal Digit to Floating Point

Function: A single decimal digit is placed in temporary binary floating point format.

Input: Upon entry AL contains the value of the digit.

Output: Upon entry and exit the address of the temporary binary floating point result is in DI.

Registers used: AL, CX, and DI are modified.

Segments referenced: Upon entry the data segment contains storage for the temporary binary floating point number.

Routines called: None

Special notes: This is a near procedure needed by FPIN.

```
;ROUTINE TO PLACE DIGIT IN TEMP FLOATING POINT

fpindigit       proc    near

;clear the number first
        push    di              ; save pointer
        push    ax              ; save digit
        mov     al,0            ; zero byte
        mov     cx,13           ; do 13 bytes
fpindigit1:
        mov     [di],al         ; clear the byte
        inc     di              ; point to next byte
        loop    fpindigit1      ; loop for more
        pop     ax              ; restore digit
        pop     di              ; restore pointer

;move the digit into place
        mov     [di+9],al       ; place the digit

        ret                     ; return

fpindigit       endp
```

FPTNORM

Normalization of Temporary Floating Point

Function: This routine normalizes temporary binary floating numbers that have too large a mantissa.

Input: Upon entry DS:DI points to a temporary binary floating point number whose mantissa is too large.

Output: Upon exit DS:DI points to a normalized temporary binary floating point number.

Registers used: No registers are modified. DI must point to the number.

Segments referenced: The data segment must contain the temporary floating number.

Routines called: None

Special notes: Equates are used to shorten address fields. This is a near procedure needed by FPIN.

```
; ROUTINE TO NORMALIZE TEMP FLOATING POINT NUMBERS THAT HAVE
; TOO LARGE A MANTISSA
;
fptnorm proc    near
;
        cmp     diword+8,100h   ; test if too high
        jl      fptnorm1        ; exit if low enough
        sar     diword+8,1      ; shift right all bytes
        rcr     diword+6,1      ; carry on
        rcr     diword+4,1
        rcr     diword+2,1
        rcr     diword+0,1
        inc     diword+11       ; increment exponent
        jmp     fptnorm
;
fptnorm1:       ret             ; return
;
fptnorm endp
```

Multiplication of Temporary Floating Point Number by 10

Function: A temporary binary floating number is multiplied by 10. The result is not normalized.

Input: Upon entry DS:DI points to a temporary binary floating point number.

Output: Upon exit DS:DI points to a temporary binary floating point number. This number is not normalized.

Registers used: AX, CX, DX, and DI are modified. DI is used to point to the input.

Segments referenced: The data segment contains the temporary binary floating point number.

Routines called: None

Special notes: This is a near routine needed by FPIN.

```
;ROUTINE TO MULTIPLY TEMP FLOATING POINT BY 10

fptmul  proc    near

        mov     cx,5            ; for a count of 5
        mov     dx,0            ; carry of zero
fptmul1:
        push    cx              ; save count
        mov     ax,dx           ; previous carry
        xchg    ax,[di]         ; switch with 16-bit digit
        mov     cx,10           ; multiplier of 10
        mul     cx              ; multiply
        add     [di],ax         ; add into carry in place
        add     di,2            ; next 16-bit digit
        pop     cx              ; restore count
        loop    fptmul1

        ret                     ; return

fptmul  endp
```

FPTDIV

Division of Temporary Floating Point Number by 10

FUNCTION: This routine divides a temporary binary floating point number by 10.

Input: Upon entry DS:DI points to a temporary binary floating point number.

Output: Upon exit DS:DI points to a temporary binary floating point number.

Registers used: AX, CX, DX, and DI are modified. DI is used to point to the input.

Segments referenced: The data segment contains a temporary binary floating point number.

Routines called: None

Special notes: Equates are used to shorten address fields. This routine is needed by FPIN.

```
; ROUTINE TO DIVIDE TEMP FLOATING POINT NUMBER BY 1Ø -- RESULT IS
; NOT NORMALIZED
;
fptdiv  proc    near
;
; shift mantissa by 4 places
        mov     cx,4            ; for a count of 4
fptdiv1:
        sal     diword+Ø,1      ; shift all digits left
        rcl     diword+2,1      ; carry on
        rcl     diword+4,1
        rcl     diword+6,1
        rcl     diword+8,1
        dec     diword+11
        loop    fptdiv1
;
; divide mantissa by 1Ø
        mov     cx,5            ; 5 words in number
        mov     dx,Ø            ; previous remainder
        add     di,8            ; point to end
```

```
ptdiv2:
        push    cx              ; save count
        mov     ax,[di]         ; get 16-bit digit
        mov     cx,10           ; divisor of 10
        div     cx              ; divide
        mov     [di],ax         ; put 16-bit digit back
        sub     di,2            ; next 16-bit digit
        pop     cx              ; restore count
        loop    fptdiv2

        ret                     ; return

ptdiv   endp
```

FPIN

Conversion from External to Internal Floating Point

Function: This routine accepts an ASCII decimal floating number from a standard input device and converts it to internal binary floating point.

Input: The characters of the floating point number are received in ASCII through a call to a standard input routine. The decimal floating point number has an optional sign, followed by decimal digits of the mantissa with one embedded decimal point. Following the mantissa is an option exponent which starts with the letter E, then an optional sign, then a decimal number. It is possible to get erroneous results if the number is too large or small to be stored as a single precision binary floating point number (see Figure 5-4).

Output: Upon exit a single precision binary floating point number is in SFPBUFF. The single precision floating point number has a 24-bit binary mantissa, a sign bit, and an 8-bit exponent biased by 128 (see Figure 5-3).

Registers used: No registers are modified.

Segments referenced: The data segment contains the variables FPTEMP1, FPTEMP2, and SFPBUFF.

Routines called: STDIN, FPINDIGIT, FPTMUL, FPTDIV, and FPTNORM

Special notes: Equates are used to shorten address fields.

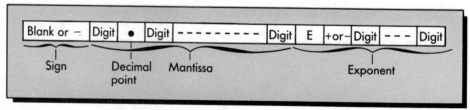

Figure 5-4.   External floating point format

```
; ROUTINE TO CONVERT FROM ASCII EXTERNAL TO INTERNAL FLOATING POINT
;
fpin    proc    far
;
        push    di              ; save registers
        push    si
```

```
        push    dx
        push    cx
        push    ax

clear fp temp1 buffer
        lea     di,fptemp1      ; point to fptemp1
        mov     al,Ø            ; digit = Ø
        call    fpindigit       ; store digit

clear the decimal flag and the count
        mov     decflag,Ø       ; clear flag
        mov     decexp,Ø        ; clear decimal exponent

look for the sign
        call    stdin           ; look for sign
        cmp     al,'-'          ; minus
        jz      fpin1           ; store it
        cmp     al,'+'          ; plus
        jz      fpin2           ; ignore it
        jmp     fpin3           ; anything else gets used

fpin1:
set sign as negative
        mov     fptemp1b1Ø,8Øh  ; put sign in place

fpin2:
        call    stdin           ; get next digit
fpin3:
        cmp     al,'.'          ; check for decimal place
        jne     fpin4           ; go on if not

set decimal flag
        cmp     decflag,Ø       ; decimal flag already set?
        jne     fpin5           ; exit if not the first
        mov     decflag,ØFFh    ; set it now
        jmp     fpin2           ; go back for a digit

fpin4:
        sub     al,3Øh          ; subtract 3Øh
        jl      fpin5           ; too low?
        cmp     al,9
        jg      fpin5           ; too high?
        jmp     fpin6           ; got a digit

fpin5:
        jmp     fpin15          ; end of mantissa
```

```
;
; load digit as a floating point number
fpin6:
        lea     di,fptemp2      ; point to fptemp2
        call    fpindigit       ; put in the digit
;
; multiply result by 1Ø
        lea     di,fptemp1      ; point to fptemp1
        call    fptmul          ; multiply by 1Ø
;
; pick one with larger exponent
        mov     cx,fptemp1w11   ; get sign of fptemp1
        sub     cx,fptemp2w11   ; subtract sign of fptemp2
        je      fpin11          ; skip if equal
        jg      fpin9           ; if exp fptemp2 is less
;
fpin7:
; exponent of fptemp1 is less than exponent of fptemp2
        neg     cx              ; absolute value of exp
fpin8:
; shift the bits
        sar     fptemp1w8,1     ; shift all bits right
        rcr     fptemp1w6,1     ; carry on
        rcr     fptemp1w4,1
        rcr     fptemp1w2,1
        rcr     fptemp1wØ,1
        loop    fpin8
;
; set the exponent
        mov     ax,fptemp2w11   ; get exp of fptemp2
        mov     fptemp1w11,ax   ; put in exp of fptemp1
;
        jmp     fpin11          ; done with this case
;
fpin9:
;
; exponent of fptemp2 is less than exponent of fptemp1
;
fpin1Ø:
; shift the bits
        sar     fptemp2w8,1     ; shift all bits right
        rcr     fptemp2w6,1     ; carry on
        rcr     fptemp2w4,1
        rcr     fptemp2w2,1
        rcr     fptemp2wØ,1
        loop    fpin1Ø
;
; set the exponent
        mov     ax,fptemp1w11   ; get exp of fptemp1
        mov     fptemp2w11,ax   ; put in exp of fptemp2
```

```
        jmp      fpin11            ; end of this case

fpin11:

;  add the digit to the result

        mov      cx,5              ; for a count of 5 words
        lea      di,fptemp1        ; di points to fptemp1
        lea      si,fptemp2        ; si points to fptemp2
        clc
fpin12:
        mov      ax,[si]           ; get 16-bit digit from fptemp1
        inc      si                ; point to next 16-bit digit
        inc      si
        adc      [di],ax           ; add to 16-bit digit of fptemp2
        inc      di                ; point to next 16-bit digit
        inc      di
        loop     fpin12

;  normalize
        lea      di,fptemp1        ; point to fptemp1
        call     fptnorm           ; renormalize it

fpin13:
;
;  decrement decimal exponent if dec flag is on
        cmp      decflag,Ø         ; check decimal flag
        je       fpin14            ; skip if not set
        dec      decexp            ; dec exponent if set
;
fpin14:
        jmp      fpin2             ; go back for next digit
;
fpin15:
;  adjust for the decimal point
        add      al,3Øh            ; restore ASCII
        and      al,5Fh            ; upper or lower case
        cmp      al,'E'            ; is it E for exponent?
        jne      fpin16
;
;  grab exponent
;
        call     sgndec16in        ; get signed decimal exponent
        add      decexp,dx         ; add it to our current value
;
fpin16:
;  check for sign of decimal exponent
        mov      cx,decexp         ; get decimal exponent
        cmp      cx,Ø              ; check its sign
        jg       fpin17            ; if positive
```

```
              jl      fpin18           ; if negative
;
; zero count
              jmp     fpin20           ; done if exponent is zero
;
; positive decimal exponent
fpin17:
              push cx                   ; save count = decimal exponent
;
; multiply result by 10
              lea     di,fptemp1       ; point to fptemp1
              call    fptmul           ; mutiply by 10
;
; normalize
              lea     di,fptemp1       ; point to fptemp1
              call    fptnorm          ; renormalize it
;
              pop     cx               ; restore the count
              loop    fpin17
;
              jmp     fpin20           ; end of this case
;
fpin18:
; negative count
              neg     cx               ; absolute value of exponent
fpin19:
              push    cx               ; save the count = exponent
;
; divide mantissa by 10
              lea     di,fptemp1       ; point to fptemp1
              call    fptdiv           ; divide by 10
;
; normalize
              lea     di,fptemp1       ; point to fptemp1
              call    fptnorm          ; renormalize it
;
              pop     cx               ; restore the count
              loop    fpin19
;
fpin20:
              call    tfp2sfp          ; convert to single precision
;
              pop     ax               ; restore registers
              pop     cx
              pop     dx
              pop     si
              pop     di
              ret                      ; return
;
fpin    endp
```

Floating Point Output

The main routine of this section converts from internal single precision binary floating point to external decimal floating point. As in the previous section, there are a number of support routines to perform the key steps of the conversion algorithm. Again, these routines are "near" procedures, and are designed to work with prevailing conditions within the main conversion routine. Also, each routine has a full header to better explain its function.

SFP2TFP

Conversion from Single Precision to Temporary Floating Point

Function: This routine converts a single precision binary floating point number into a temporary binary floating point number.

Input: Upon entry a single precision floating point number is stored in SFPBUFF. The single precision floating point number has a 24-bit binary mantissa, a sign bit, and an 8-bit exponent biased by 128 (see Figure 5-3).

Output: Upon exit a temporary binary floating point number is stored in FPTEMP1. The temporary binary floating point number has a 72-bit binary mantissa with 8 bits to the left of these for internal use, a sign byte, and a 16-bit two's complement binary exponent (see Figure 5-2).

Registers used: AX is modified.

Segments referenced: The data segment contains the variables SFPBUFF and FPTEMP1.

Routines called: None

Special notes: Equates are used to shorten address fields. This is a near procedure needed by FPOUT.

```
; ROUTINE TO CONVERT FROM SINGLE PRECISION FLOATING POINT
; TO TEMP FLOATING POINT
;
sfp2tfp proc    near
```

```
;
; clear lower part of mantissa
        mov     fptemp1w0,0     ; clear word
        mov     fptemp1w2,0     ; clear word
        mov     fptemp1w4,0     ; clear word
;
; move rest of mantissa
        mov     ax,sfpbuffw0    ; low 2 bytes
        mov     fptemp1w6,ax    ; put in place
;
        mov     ax,sfpbuffw2    ; high 7 bits
        and     ax,007Fh        ; remove sign
        or      ax,0080h        ; restore msb
        mov     fptemp1w8,ax    ; put in place
;
; move sign
        mov     al,sfpbuffb2    ; in upper byte
        and     al,80h          ; just sign bit
        mov     fptemp1b10,al   ; byte 10 of fptemp1
;
; move exponent
        mov     al,sfpbuffb3    ; byte 3 of sfp
        mov     ah,0            ; make into a word
        sub     ax,80h          ; remove bias
        mov     fptemp1w11,ax   ; its 16-bit 2's comp
;
        ret                     ; return
;
sfp2tfp endp
```

Display of Floating Point

Function: This routine displays a floating point number on the standard output device.

Input: Upon input a number is stored in temporary decimal floating point form. The temporary format has a string of 25 decimal digits, a sign byte, and a base ten exponent which is stored in two's complement 16-bit binary format (see Figure 5-5).

Output: The individual characters of a floating point number are sent out the standard output device. The form of the output is: a sign character which is blank or minus, followed by decimal digits of the mantissa with one embedded decimal point to the right of the first significant digit. Following the mantissa is an exponent which starts with the letter E, then a sign, then a decimal number (see Figure 5-4).

Registers used: AL, CX, DX, and SI are modified.

Segments referenced: The data segment contains the variables DECBUFF (25 bytes), DECSIGN (1 byte), and DECEXP (2 bytes).

Routines called: STDOUT

Special notes: This is a near procedure needed by FPOUT.

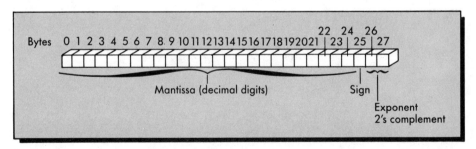

Figure 5-5.   Temporary decimal floating point

```
ROUTINE TO DISPLAY TEMPORARY DECIMAL FLOATING POINT NUMBERS

decshow         proc    near

output the sign
        cmp     decsign,Ø       ; is the sign there?
```

```
                mov     al,' '              ; space if not
                je      tdecshow1
;
; output a minus sign
                mov     al,'-'              ; minus sign
tdecshow1:
                call    stdout              ; send it out
;
tdecshow2:
; output the first digit and a decimal point
                lea     si,decbuff+21       ; point to first digit
                mov     al,[si]             ; get it
                dec     si                  ; point to next digit
                add     al,30h              ; make it ASCII
                call    stdout              ; send it out
;
                mov     al,'.'              ; ASCII decimal point
                call    stdout              ; send it out
;
; output the rest of the decimal string
                mov     cx,7                ; only 7 more digits
tdecshow3:
                mov     al,[si]             ; get digit
                dec     si                  ; point to next digit
                add     al,30h              ; make ASCII
                call    stdout              ; send it out
                loop    tdecshow3
;
                mov     al,'E'              ; E for exponent
                call    stdout              ; send it out
;
; now the exponent
                mov     dx,decexp           ; grab exponent
                cmp     dx,0                ; check sign
                mov     al,'+'              ; plus sign
                jge     tdecshow4           ; if nonnegative
;
; if negative exponent
                neg     dx                  ; absolute value of exponent
                mov     al,'-'              ; minus sign
;
tdecshow4:
                call    stdout              ; output sign of exponent
                call    dec16out            ; output exponent
;
                ret                         ; return
;
tdecshow         endp
```

BIN802DEC

Conversion from 80-Bit Binary to Decimal Digits

Function: This routine converts an 80-bit binary integer into a decimal string.

Input: Upon entry SI points to an 80-bit binary integer to be used as input and DI points to a 25-digit decimal string to be used as output (see Figure 5-6).

Output: Upon exit a 25-digit decimal string is where DI pointed upon entry. DI still points there upon exit (see Figure 5-7).

Registers used: AX, BX, CX, DX, and SI are modified. DI is used to point to the output, but is preserved.

Segments referenced: The data segment contains storage for the 80-bit binary number (10 bytes) and the 25-digit decimal number (25 bytes).

Routines called: None

Special notes: This is a near procedure needed by FPOUT.

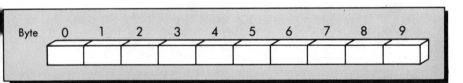

Figure 5-6.   80-bit binary integer

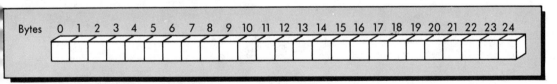

Figure 5-7.   25-digit decimal string

```
; ROUTINE TO CONVERT 80-BIT BINARY NUMBER INTO A DECIMAL STRING
;
bin802dec        proc    near
;
; clear the string
        push    di              ; save destination pointer
```

```
;
        mov     al,Ø            ; zero byte
        mov     cx,25           ; for a count of 25
bin8Ø2dec1:
        mov     [di],al         ; zero the byte
        inc     di              ; point to next byte
        loop    bin8Ø2dec1
;
        pop     di              ; restore destination pointer
;
; loop forever
;
bin8Ø2dec2:
        push    si              ; save source pointer
;
; divide mantissa by 1Ø
        mov     bx,Ø            ; done flag
        mov     cx,5            ; 5 words in number
        mov     dx,Ø            ; previous remainder
        add     si,8            ; point to high end
;
bin8Ø2dec3:
        push    cx              ; save count
        mov     ax,[si]         ; get 16-bit digit
        mov     cx,1Ø           ; divisor of 1Ø
        div     cx              ; divide
        mov     [si],ax         ; put 16-bit digit back
        or      bx,ax           ; check for zero
        sub     si,2            ; point to next 16-bit digit
        pop     cx              ; restore count
        loop    bin8Ø2dec3
;
        mov     [di],dl         ; remainder is decimal digit
        inc     di              ; point to next decimal digit
;
        pop     si              ; restore source pointer
        cmp     bx,Ø            ; was the binary zero?
        jnz     bin8Ø2dec2      ; loop if nonzero
;
        ret                     ; return
bin8Ø2dec       endp
```

DECNORM

Normalization of Temporary Decimal Floating Point

Function: This routine normalizes a temporary decimal floating point number.

Input: Upon entry DS:DI points to a temporary decimal floating point number.

Output: Upon exit the temporary floating point number is normalized.

Registers used: AX, CX, and DI are modified.

Segments referenced: The data segment contains storage for a temporary decimal floating point number.

Routines called: None

Special notes: Equates are used to shorten address fields.

```
ROUTINE TO NORMALIZE TEMPORARY DECIMAL FLOATING POINT NUMBER

ecnorm proc     near

check top+1 digit
        cmp     dibyte+22,Ø     ; is it already zero?
        je      decnorm2        ; if so exit

round up starting with bottom digit
        mov     al,[di]         ; first digit
        add     al,al           ; double it for rounding
        mov     ah,Ø            ; prepare carry
        aaa                     ; adjust for decimal

now shift the rest
        mov     cx,24           ; for a count of 24
ecnorm1:
        mov     al,[di+1]       ; get next digit
        add     al,ah           ; add carry
        mov     ah,Ø            ; prepare next carry
        aaa                     ; adjust for decimal
        mov     [di],al         ; put digit in place
        inc     di              ; point to next digit
        loop    decnorm1
```

```
;
        inc    decexp         ; increment decimal exponent
;
decnorm2:
        ret                   ; return
;
decnorm endp
```

DECHALF

Halving a Temporary Decimal Floating Point Number

Function: This routine divides a temporary decimal floating point number by two.

Input: Upon input DI points to a temporary decimal floating point number.

Output: Upon exit the number has been divided by two. The result is not normalized.

Registers used: AX, CX, and DI are modified.

Segments referenced: The data segment contains a temporary decimal floating point number.

Routines called: None

Special notes: This is a near procedure needed by FPOUT.

```
ROUTINE TO DIVIDE TEMPORARY DECIMAL NUMBER BY 2 - RESULT NOT NORMED

echalf proc    near

first shift up one digit
        mov    cx,25        ; for a count of 25
        mov    al,0         ; zero previous digit
echalf1:
        xchg   al,[di]      ; exchange with current digit
        inc    di           ; point to next digit
        loop   dechalf1

        dec    decexp       ; decrement decimal digit

now divide by 2
        mov    cx,25        ; for a count of 25
        mov    ah,0         ; clear
echalf2:
        push   cx           ; save count
        dec    di           ; point to next digit
        mov    al,[di]      ; get the digit
        mov    cl,2         ; divisor of 2
        aad                 ; adjust for division
```

```
        div     cl              ; divide
        mov     [di],al         ; put back
        pop     cx              ; restore count
        loop    dechalf2
;
        ret                     ; return
;
dechalf endp
```

DECDOUBLE

Doubling a Temporary Decimal Floating Point Number

Function: This routine multiplies a temporary decimal floating point number by two.

Input: Upon entry DS:DI points to a temporary decimal floating point number.

Output: Upon exit the number has been doubled.

Registers used: AX, CX, and DI are modified.

Segments referenced: The data segment contains storage for the temporary decimal floating point number.

Routines called: None

Special notes: This is a near procedure needed by FPOUT.

```
ROUTINE TO MULTIPLY TEMPORARY DECIMAL NUMBER BY 2 - RESULT NOT NORMED

decdouble       proc    near

        mov     cx, 25          ; for a count of 25
        mov     ah, Ø           ; clear previous carry
decdouble1:
        mov     al, [di]        ; get digit
        sal     al, 1           ; multiply by 2
        add     al, ah          ; add the carry
        aam                     ; adjust for decimal multiplication
        mov     [di], al        ; put back the byte
        inc     di              ; point to next byte
        loop    decdouble1

        ret                     ; return

decdouble       endp
```

FPOUT

Conversion from Internal to External Floating Point

Function: This routine displays a single precision floating point number on the standard output device as a decimal floating point number.

Input: Upon entry a single precision binary floating point number is in SFPBUFF. The single precision floating point number has a 24-bit binary mantissa, a sign bit, and an 8-bit exponent biased by 128 (see Figure 5-3).

Output: The individual characters of a decimal floating number are sent out through the standard output device. The decimal floating point number has a sign character which is blank or minus, followed by decimal digits of the mantissa with one embedded decimal point to the right of the first significant digit. Following the mantissa is an exponent which starts with the letter E, then a sign, then a decimal number (see Figure 5-4).

Registers used: AX, CX, BX, DX, SI, and DI are modified.

Segments referenced: The data segment contains storage for the variables DECBUFF, DECSIGN, DECEXP, FPTEMP1, and SFPBUFF.

Routines called: STDOUT, SFP2TFP, DECHALF, DECDOUBLE, DECNORM, TDECSHOW.

Special notes: Equates are used to shorten address fields.

```
; ROUTINE TO CONVERT FROM INTERNAL FLOATING POINT
; TO ASCII FLOATING POINT
;
fpout   proc    far
;
        push    di              ; save registers
        push    si
        push    dx
        push    bx
        push    cx
        push    ax
```

check for zero as a special case

```
        mov     ax,sfpbuffw0    ; get low word
        or      ax,sfpbuffw2    ; get high word
        jnz     fpout1          ; go on if not zero

        mov     al,'0'          ; make a zero
        call    stdout          ; send it out
        jmp     fpout6          ; and exit
```

fpout1:

convert from single precision to temp floating point

```
        call    sfp2tfp         ; convert to temp format
```

initialize exponent for unnormed position

```
        mov     decexp,21       ; exp = 21 for start
```

set the sign

```
        mov     al,fptemp1b10   ; get sign
        mov     decsign,al      ; put it away
```

convert mantissa to a decimal string

```
        lea     si,fptemp1      ; si points to fptemp1
        lea     di,decbuff      ; di points to decbuff
        call    bin802dec       ; make decimal string
```

check sign of binary exponent

```
        mov     cx,fptemp1w11   ; get the binary exp
        sub     cx,72           ; biased by -72
        cmp     cx,0            ; check its sign
        jl      fpout2          ; if negative
        jg      fpout4          ; if positive
        jmp     fpout5          ; if zero
```

fpout2:

binary exponent is negative

```
        neg     cx              ; absolute value of exp
```

fpout3:

```
        push    cx              ; save count = binary exp
```

divide by 2

```
        lea     di,decbuff      ; point to decbuff
        call    dechalf         ; divide by 2
```

normalize

```
        lea     di,decbuff      ; point to decbuff
        call    decnorm         ; renormalize
```

```
;
        pop     cx              ; restore count
        loop    fpout3
;
        jmp     fpout5          ; end of case
;
; binary exponent is positive
;
fpout4:
        push    cx              ; save count = binary exp
;
; multiply by 2
        lea     di,decbuff      ; point to decbuff
        call    decdouble       ; multiply by 2
;
; normalize
        lea     di,decbuff      ; point to decbuff
        call    decnorm         ; renormalize
;
        pop     cx              ; restore count
        loop    fpout4
;
        jmp     fpout5          ; end of case
;
fpout5:
; output the number
        call    tdecshow        ; display the number
;
fpout6:
        pop     ax              ; restore registers
        pop     cx
        pop     bx
        pop     dx
        pop     si
        pop     di
        ret                     ; return
;
fpout   endp
```

This section contains routines to convert between single and double binary floating point formats and 16-bit binary integer formats. The routines to convert between integer and floating point representations have the familiar names FIX and FLOAT because they perform exactly the same actions as these well-known functions in FORTRAN and other languages.

Each routine in this section stands alone without support routines.

Conversion from Internal Floating Point to 16-Bit Integer

Function: This routine converts from internal single precision binary floating point to internal 16-bit signed two's complement integer.

Input: Upon entry a single precision binary floating point is in SFPBUFF. The single precision floating point number has a 24-bit binary mantissa, a sign bit, and an 8-bit exponent biased by 128 (see Figure 5-3).

Output: Upon exit a 16-bit signed two's complement binary number is in the DX register.

Registers used: Only DX is modified. It is used for output.

Segments referenced: The data segment contains storage for SFPBUFF.

Routines called: None

Special notes: Equates are used to shorten address fields.

```
ROUTINE TO CONVERT FROM INTERNAL FLOATING POINT
TO INTERNAL INTEGER (truncate)

x     proc    far

the number is in sfpbuff

      push    cx              ; save registers
      push    ax
```

```
;
; get the mantissa
        mov     ax,sfpbuffwØ    ; AX gets low part
        mov     dx,sfpbuffw2    ; DX gets high part
        and     dx,ØØ7Fh        ; just the mantissa
        or      dx,ØØ8Øh        ; restore the msb
;
; get the exponent
        mov     cl,sfpbuffb3    ; get the exponent
        mov     ch,Ø            ; extend to 16-bit
        sub     cx,88h          ; subtract bias+
        cmp     cx,Ø            ; check its sign
        jl      fix1            ; if negative
        jg      fix3            ; if positive
        je      fix4            ; if zero
;
fix1:
; shift right
        neg     cx              ; absolute value
fix2:
        sar     dx,1            ; shift all bits right
        rcr     ax,1            ; carry on
        loop    fix2
;
        jmp     fix4            ; end of case
;
; shift left
fix3:
        sal     ax,1            ; shift all bits left
        rcl     dx,1            ; carry on
        loop    fix3
;
        jmp     fix4            ; end of case
;
fix4:
; check the sign
        mov     al,sfpbuffb2    ; get sign
        and     al,8Øh          ; just bit 7
        jz      fix5            ; is it on?
        neg     dx              ; 2's comp if neg
fix5:
        pop     ax              ; restore registers
        pop     cx
        ret                     ; return
;
fix     endp
```

Conversion from 16-Bit Integer to Floating Point

Function: This routine converts an unsigned 16-bit binary number to a single precision binary floating point number.

Input: Upon entry DX contains an unsigned 16-bit binary number.

Output: Upon exit SFPBUFF contains a single precision floating point number. The single precision floating point number has a 24-bit binary mantissa, a sign bit, and an 8-bit exponent biased by 128 (see Figure 5-3).

Registers used: No registers are modified. DX is used for input.

Segments referenced: The data segment contains storage for the variable SFPBUFF and the message INTERNAL.

Routines called: MESSOUT, HEX16OUT, STDSPACE (all for debugging)

Special notes: Equates are used to shorten address fields.

```
ROUTINE TO CONVERT FROM INTERNAL INTEGER TO INTERNAL FLOATING POINT

loat    proc    far

the number is in DX

        push    dx                  ; save registers
        push    cx
        push    ax

        mov     ax,Ø                ; extend to 32 bits
        cmp     dx,Ø                ; check if zero
        jz      float4

loat1:
        mov     cx,98ØØh            ; initialize exponent and sign
 shift left until normalized
loat2:
        test    ax,ØØ8Øh            ; done yet?
        jnz     float3             ; exit if so
        sal     dx,1               ; shift all bits left if not
```

```
        rcl     ax,1            ; carry on
        dec     ch              ; decrement the exponent
        jmp     float2
;
float3:
;
; pack it in
        and     ax,007Fh        ; just the mantissa
        or      ax,cx           ; exponent and sign
;
float4:
        mov     sfpbuffw0,dx    ; put lower part into place
        mov     sfpbuffw2,ax    ; put upper part into place
;
; show hex for debugging
        lea     si,internal     ; point to message
        call    stdmessout      ; send message
;
        mov     dx,sfpbuffw2    ; upper word
        call    hex16out        ; show it
;
        mov     dx,sfpbuffw0    ; lower word
        call    hex16out        ; show it
;
        call    stdspace        ; skip space
;

        pop     ax              ; restore registers
        pop     cx
        pop     dx
        ret                     ; return
;
float   endp
```

SFP2DFP

Conversion from Single to Double Precision

Function: This routine converts an internal single precision binary floating point number to an internal double precision floating point number.

Input: Upon entry a single precision binary floating point number is in SFPBUFF. The single precision floating point number has a 24-bit binary mantissa, a sign bit, and an 8-bit exponent biased by 128 (see Figure 5-3).

Output: Upon exit a double precision binary floating point number is in DFPBUFF. The double precision floating point number has a 40-bit binary mantissa, a sign bit, and an 8-bit exponent biased by 128 (see Figure 5-8).

Registers used: No registers are modified.

Segments referenced: The data segment contains storage for the variables SFPBUFF and DFPBUFF.

Routines called: None

Special notes: Equates are used to shorten address fields.

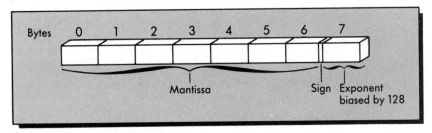

Figure 5-8. Double precision binary floating point

```
ROUTINE TO CONVERT FROM INTERNAL SINGLE PRECISION
TO INTERNAL DOUBLE PRECISION FLOATING POINT

sfp2dfp proc     far

        push    ax              ; save registers
```

```
;
; clear low part of mantissa
        mov     dfpbuffwØ,Ø     ; clear low word
        mov     dfpbuffw2,Ø     ; clear next low word
;
; move rest of number
        mov     ax,sfpbuffwØ    ; get word from single precision
        mov     dfpbuffw4,ax    ; put in double precision
;
        mov     ax,sfpbuffw2    ; get word from single precision
        mov     dfpbuffw6,ax    ; put in double precision
;
        pop     ax              ; restore registers
        ret                     ; return
;
sfp2dfp endp
```

Conversion from Double to Single Precision

Function: This routine converts an internal double precision binary floating point number to an internal single precision floating point number.

Input: Upon entry a double precision binary floating point number is in DFPBUFF. The double precision floating point number has a 40-bit binary mantissa, a sign bit, and an 8-bit exponent biased by 128 (see Figure 5-8).

Output: Upon exit a single precision binary floating point number is in SFPBUFF. The single precision floating point number has a 24-bit binary mantissa, a sign bit, and an 8-bit exponent biased by 128 (see Figure 5-3).

Registers used: No registers are modified.

Segments referenced: The data segment contains storage for the variables SFPBUFF and DFPBUFF.

Routines called: None

Special notes: Equates are used to shorten address fields.

```
ROUTINE TO CONVERT FROM INTERNAL DOUBLE PRECISION
TO INTERNAL SINGLE PRECISION FLOATING POINT

p2sfp proc    far

      push    ax              ; save registers

      mov     ax,dfpbuffw4    ; get word from double precision
      mov     sfpbuffw0,ax    ; place in single precision

      mov     ax,dfpbuffw6    ; get word from double precision
      mov     sfpbuffw2,ax    ; place in single precision

      pop     ax              ; restore registers
      ret                     ; return

p2sfp endp
```

Multidigit Arithmetic

*T*he routines in this chapter perform the four fundamental arithmetic operations of addition, subtraction, multiplication, and division upon multidigit integers.

Large capacity integers can be constructed by chaining together several smaller 8-bit or 16-bit integers, with each 8-bit or 16-bit integer piece acting as a digit of the number. Hence the name *multidigit integer* is used to describe these large-sized integers. In this chapter we use 16-bit integers as "digits" in our routines, but these routines can easily be modified to use 8-bit integers instead.

Multidigit binary integers are useful in applications requiring a high degree of precision. These include pure and applied mathematics. For example, there are some famous numbers such as pi or e whose digit patterns are the subject of mathematical research, and there are some very large prime numbers whose existence is of interest (see "The Search for Prime Numbers" by Carl Pomerance, *Scientific American*, December 1982). Often, searches for these large numbers are used merely as tests for machines and programmers, but a very important application for large primes and for large integers in general is the encryption of sensitive computer data. In fact, encrypting and decrypting algorithms require multidigit operations such as those presented in this chapter.

Many operations on these larger-sized integers can be accomplished by combining 8-bit or 16-bit arithmetic operations that work on the individual 8-bit or 16-bit "digits". The methods for combining these digit-by-digit operations are pretty much the same methods that are taught in elementary school for dealing with multidigit decimal arithmetic. You can see this in the addition, subtraction, and multiplication routines included in this chapter. The one exception to this is our division routine. It uses binary arithmetic to greatly simplify the "guessing process" normally used in long division of decimal numbers.

MBINADD

Multidigit Binary Addition

Function: This routine adds two multidigit binary numbers.

Input: Upon entry DS:SI points to the first number, DS:DI points to the second number, and DS:BX points to the location where the result will be stored. The size of these multidigit numbers is controlled by the constant ISIZE. All three numbers contain 16*ISIZE number of bits and are stored in ISIZE number of 16-bit words of memory.

Output: Upon exit DS:BX points to where the result is stored.

Registers Used: No registers are modified.

Segments Referenced: Upon entry the data segment must contain storage for three multidigit numbers, two for input and one for output.

Routines Called: None

Special Notes: None

```
; ROUTINE TO ADD MULTIDIGIT BINARY NUMBERS
;
mbinadd proc    far
;
        push    si              ; save registers
        push    di
        push    bx
        push    cx
        push    ax
;
        mov     cx,isize        ; get the number of 16-bit "digits"
        clc                     ; clear the carry in
mbinadd1:
        mov     ax,[si]         ; get "digit" from first number
        inc     si              ; point to next "digit"
        inc     si
        adc     ax,[di]         ; add "digit" from second number
        inc     di              ; point to next "digit"
        inc     di
        mov     [bx],ax         ; move resulting "digit" into place
        inc     bx              ; point to next "digit"
        inc     bx
```

```
        loop    mbinadd1        ; loop through all "digits"

        pop     ax              ; restore registers
        pop     cx
        pop     bx
        pop     di
        pop     si
        ret

inadd endp
```

Multidigit Binary Subtraction

Function: This routine subtracts two multidigit binary numbers.

Input: Upon entry DS:SI points to the first number, DS:DI points to the second number, and DS:BX points to the location where the result of subtracting the first from the second will be stored. The size of these multidigit numbers is controlled by the constant ISIZE. All three numbers contain 16*ISIZE number of bits and are stored in ISIZE number of 16-bit words of memory.

Output: Upon exit DS:BX points to where the result is stored.

Registers Used: No registers are modified.

Segments Referenced: Upon entry the data segment must contain storage for three multidigit numbers, two for input and one for output.

Routines Called: None

Special Notes: None

```
; ROUTINE TO SUBTRACT MULTIDIGIT BINARY NUMBERS
;
mbinsub proc    far
;
        push    si              ; save registers
        push    di
        push    bx
        push    cx
        push    ax
;
        mov     cx,isize        ; get the number of 16-bit "digits"
        clc                     ; clear the carry
mbinsub1:
        mov     ax,[di]         ; get "digit" from second number
        inc     di              ; point to next "digit"
        inc     di
        sbb     ax,[si]         ; subtract "digit" of first number
        inc     si              ; point to next "digit"
        inc     si
        mov     [bx],ax         ; move resulting "digit" into place
```

```
        inc     bx              ; point to next "digit"
        inc     bx
        loop    mbinsub1        ; loop through all "digits"

        pop     ax              ; restore registers
        pop     cx
        pop     bx
        pop     di
        pop     si
        ret

insub endp
```

Multidigit Binary Multiplication

Function: This routine multiplies two multidigit binary numbers.

Input: Upon entry DS:SI points to the first number, DS:DI points to the second number, and DS:BX points to the location where the result will be stored. The size of these multidigit numbers is controlled by the constant ISIZE. The input numbers contain 16*ISIZE number of bits and the output number has double that precision. Both inputs are stored in ISIZE number of 16-bit words of memory and the output is stored in 2*ISIZE number of 16-bit words of memory.

Output: Upon exit DS:BX points to where the result is stored.

Registers Used: No registers are modified.

Segments Referenced: Upon entry the data segment must contain storage for three multidigit numbers, two for input and one for output.

Routines Called: None

Special Notes: None

```
; ROUTINE TO MULTIPLY MULTIDIGIT BINARY NUMBERS
;
mbinmul proc    far
;
        push    si              ; save registers
        push    di
        push    bx
        push    cx
        push    ax
;
; clear result buffer
        push    bx              ; save result pointer BX
        mov     ax,Ø            ; get a zero
        mov     cx,2*isize      ; double precision for this number
        cld                     ; forward direction
mbinmul1:
        mov     [bx],ax         ; clear the "digit"
        inc     bx              ; point to next "digit"
        inc     bx
        loop    mbinmul1        ; loop through all "digits"
```

```
        pop     bx              ; restore result pointer BX

        mov     cx,isize        ; get the number of 16-bit "digits"
binmul2:
        push    cx              ; save count for outer loop
        mov     dx,[si]         ; get "digit" from first number
        inc     si              ; point to next "digit"
        inc     si

        push    bx              ; save registers during inner loop
        push    di

        mov     cx,isize        ; get the number of 16-bit "digits"
binmul3:
        push    cx              ; save count for inner loop
        push    dx              ; save multiplier "digit"
        mov     ax,[di]         ; get "digit" from second number
        inc     di              ; point to next "digit"
        inc     di
        mul     dx              ; multiply
        add     [bx],ax         ; add lower "digit" to result
        inc     bx              ; point to next "digit"
        inc     bx
        adc     [bx],dx         ; add upper part to result
        pop     dx              ; restore multiplier
        pop     cx              ; restore count for inner loop
        loop    mbinmul3        ; loop through all "digits" of second

        pop     di              ; restore registers
        pop     bx

        inc     bx              ; shift by one "digit"
        inc     bx
        pop     cx              ; restore count for outer loop
        loop    mbinmul2        ; loop through all "digits" of first

        pop     ax              ; restore registers
        pop     cx
        pop     bx
        pop     di
        pop     si
        ret

binmul endp
```

MBINDIV

Multidigit Binary Division

Function: This routine divides two multidigit binary numbers, producing both a quotient and remainder.

Input: Upon entry, DS:SI points to the divisor, DS:BX points to where the dividend is upon entry and where the remainder will be upon exit, and DS:DI points to the location where the quotient will be upon exit. The size of these multidigit numbers is controlled by the constant ISIZE. The divisor and quotient contain 16*ISIZE number of bits and the dividend and remainder have double that precision. Both the divisor and quotient are stored in ISIZE number of 16-bit words of memory and the dividend and remainder are stored in 2*ISIZE number of 16-bit words of memory.

Output: Upon exit DS:BX points to where the quotient is stored and DS:DI points to where the remainder is stored.

Registers Used: No registers are modified.

Segments Referenced: Upon entry the data segment must contain storage for the multidigit numbers described above.

Routines Called: None

Special Notes: None

```
; LOCAL SUBROUTINE TO COMPARE DIVISOR AGAINST DIVIDEND
;
divcmp  proc    near
;
        push    si              ; save registers
        push    di
        push    cx
;
        std                     ; backward direction
        add     si,4*isize-2    ; point to end of temp divisor
        add     di,4*isize-2    ; point to end of quotient
        mov     cx,2*isize      ; count for double precision
;
        repz    cmpsw           ; compare "digit" by "digit"
```

```
        pop     cx              ; restore registers
        pop     di
        pop     si
        ret

ivcmp   endp


; LOCAL SUBROUTINE TO ARITHMETIC SHIFT DIVISOR LEFT

ivsal   proc    near

        push    si              ; save registers
        push    cx

        mov     cx,2*isize      ; set counter
        clc                     ; clear carry in
ivsal1:
        rcl     word ptr [si],1 ; shift one word by one bit
        inc     si              ; point to next word
        inc     si
        loop    divsal1         ; loop through entire divisor

        pop     cx              ; restore registers
        pop     si
        ret

ivsal   endp


; LOCAL SUBROUTINE TO LOGICAL SHIFT DIVISOR RIGHT

ivslr   proc    near

        push    si              ; save registers
        push    cx

        add     si,4*isize-2    ; point to end of temp divisor
        mov     cx,2*isize      ; count for double precision
        clc                     ; clear carry in
divslr1:
        rcr     word ptr [si],1 ; rotate one word by one bit
        dec     si              ; point to next word
        dec     si
        loop    divslr1         ; loop through entire divisor
```

```
;
        pop     cx              ; restore registers
        pop     si
        ret
;
divslr  endp
;
;
; LOCAL SUBROUTINE TO SUBTRACT SHIFTED DIVISOR FROM DIVIDEND
;
divsub  proc    near
;
        push    si              ; save registers
        push    di
        push    cx
;
        clc                     ; clear carry in
        mov     cx,2*isize      ; set the count for double precision
divsub1:
        mov     ax,[si]         ; get word from shifted divisor
        inc     si              ; point to next word
        inc     si
        sbb     [di],ax         ; subtract from word of dividend
        inc     di              ; point to next word
        inc     di
        loop    divsub1         ; loop through all words
;
        pop     cx              ; restore registers
        pop     di
        pop     si
        ret
;
divsub  endp
;
; LOCAL SUBROUTINE TO SHIFT QUOTIENT LEFT
;
quotshl proc    near
;
        push    bx              ; save registers
        push    cx
;
        mov     cx,isize        ; count for single precision
quotshl1:
        rcl     word ptr [bx],1 ; shift word of quotient left once
        inc     bx              ; point to next word
        inc     bx
        loop    quotshl1        ; loop through entire quotient
;
        pop     cx              ; restore registers
```

```
        pop     bx
        ret

uotshl endp


; ROUTINE TO DIVIDE MULTIDIGIT BINARY NUMBERS

bindiv proc    far

        push    si              ; save registers
        push    di
        push    bx
        push    cx
        push    ax

; put single precision divisor into double precision location
        push    di              ; save dividend pointer
        lea     di,tempdiv      ; point to temporary divisor
        mov     cx,isize        ; for a count of isize
        cld                     ; forward direction
        rep     movsw           ; make the transfer

; clear upper part of double precision location
        mov     ax,Ø            ; zero word
        mov     cx,isize        ; for a count of isize
        rep     stosw           ; clear the rest of the words

; restore dividend pointer and point to temp divisor
        pop     di              ; restore dividend pointer
        lea     si,tempdiv      ; point SI to temporary divisor

; initialize shift count
        mov     cx,1            ; initial count of one

; normalize divisor
mbindiv1:
        test    msbdiv,8ØØØh    ; test msb of divisor
        jnz     mbindiv2        ; exit if normalized
        call    divsal          ; arithmetic shift left if not
        inc     cx              ; count the shift
        jmp     mbindiv1        ; keep on looping until normalized
;
; compare, subtract, shift loop
mbindiv2:
        call    divcmp          ; compare divisor against dividend
        ja      mbindiv3        ; skip if too large
        call    divsub          ; subtract if ok
        stc                     ; new bit of quotient is 1
```

```
        jmp      mbindiv4        ; jump to end of loop
;
mbindiv3:
        clc                      ; new bit of quotient is Ø
mbindiv4:
        call     quotshl         ; shift bit into the quotient
        call     divslr          ; logical shift divisor right once
        loop     mbindiv2        ; loop for next digit
;
        pop      ax              ; restore registers
        pop      cx
        pop      bx
        pop      di
        pop      si
        ret
;
mbindiv endp
```

Graphics

*T*his chapter contains routines that perform fundamental plotting jobs on the IBM PC color graphics screen. These include point plotting, line drawing, character plotting, and the filling of areas.

The need for graphics in computing has clearly been established over the past few years. The advent of personal computers with color video graphics has now made computer graphics a cost-effective alternative to the time-consuming and laborious hand-drawing of pictures.

The routines in this chapter have been carefully optimized for speed, register usage, and simplicity. Special attention has been paid to routines used most often; that is, point-plotting and line-drawing routines. The point-plotting routine in this chapter plots about 10,000 points per second, more than three times faster than the point-plotting routine in the IBM ROM BIOS.

The line-drawing routine (SETLINE) uses Bresenham's algorithm, a very popular and fast algorithm. Its critical loop consists of a call to the point-plotting routine plus a handful of 8088 instructions. Thus, optimization of point plotting is the dominant factor in optimizing the speed of this line-drawing routine. On a speed test, about 8,000 points per second were plotted using this line-drawing routine. The overhead due to the line-drawing routine itself can be reduced by a factor of two to yield about 9,000 points per second, if self-modifying code were to be used (see the routine by Dan Rollins on pages 75-77 in *Doctor Dobb's Journal*, June 1983). However, self-modifying code is not considered good programming practice, so we have refrained from it.

Box-filling routines (SETBOX and XORBOX) have been included to optimize the speed of filling large rectangular areas. These routines can fill a whole screen in about a fifth of a second (compared with 6.4 seconds for plotting every point on the screen.) If you wish to clear the whole screen, then use the routine CLS to do that in less than a tenth of a second.

For both the point-plotting and box-filling routines there are "set" and "xor" versions. The "set" versions (SETPT and SETBOX) work by overwriting previous color values in the specified pixels, whereas the "xor" versions (XORPT and XORBOX) use the XOR (exclusive OR) logical operation to combine previous color values with new color values. This is useful in constructing cursors and icons which need to move around a screen without destroying what was there before. Objects that have been placed on the screen with the XOR operation can be completely removed by placing them a second time on the screen with exactly the same position, color, and XOR operation!

Two types of characters can be plotted: stroke characters and raster characters. Stroke characters consist of a series of strokes, each drawn with the line-plotting routine. Raster characters consist of a dot matrix pattern on the screen with each "dot" drawn using the box-filling routine. Both stroke and raster characters can be plotted in any valid color value (0-3) and can be magnified by any integral amount, independently in both horizontal and vertical directions. To use the stroke character routine you must create a table of stroke characters. This gives you the flexibility to design your own character set. Raster characters use a table which is included in IBM's BIOS ROM.

A routine (GMESSOUT) is included to plot strings on the graphics screen using either stroke or raster characters. A variable FONT determines which is to be used.

As an added bonus, there is a "paint" routine (PAINT) which can be used to fill irregular areas on the screen, as does the PAINT command in IBM's Advanced BASIC (see Mitchell Waite and Christopher L. Morgan, *Graphics Primer for the IBM PC* [Berkeley: Osborne/McGraw-Hill, 1983]). The algorithm for this routine has been developed over a number of years in the computer graphics literature and by our computer graphics students at California State University, Hayward.

The algorithm for our PAINT routine uses a stack in much the same way that DOS 1 versions of IBM's PAINT algorithm do. However, starting with version 2 of its Advanced BASIC, IBM's PAINT command uses an algorithm which does not seem to use a stack to keep track of where to paint.

In general, paint routines do very well for small iregular areas, but are definitely outclassed for large regular areas by box-filling routines.

Our PAINT routine runs a bit slow, about as fast as using the IBM BIOS point-plotting routine to fill the same area, but several times slower than the paint algorithms used in IBM's Advanced BASIC. The routine could be optimized in a number of ways to increase its speed. For example, some of the byte- or word-oriented techniques used in our box-filling routines could be applied to speed it up. As it is, our routine is amazingly short and easy to understand for what it does. You would do well to carefully study it and the box-filling routines if you plan to write a faster one.

Primitive Graphics Functions

This section contains primitive graphics routines; that is, routines which do not call any others. These routines are used by all the other routines to write to and read from the screen.

Clear the Graphics Screen

Function: This routine clears the color graphics screen.

Input: None

Output: Just to the screen.

Registers Used: No registers are modified.

Segments Referenced: Upon entry ES must point to the screen RAM at B8000h.

Routines Called: None

Special Notes: None

```
; ROUTINE TO CLEAR THE GRAPHICS SCREEN
;
cls     proc    far
;
        push    cx              ; save registers
        push    ax
;
; set up the registers
        mov     cx,2000h        ; word count of whole screen
        mov     ax,0            ; zero pattern for the screen
        mov     di,ax           ; set starting address
        cld                     ; go in forward direction
;
; clear the screen with a single string operation
        rep     stosw           ; this clears the screen
;
        pop     ax              ; restore registers
        pop     cx
        ret
cls     endp
```

SETPT

Plot a Point on the Medium Resolution Color Screen

Function: This routine plots a point on the medium resolution color graphics screen. The pixel at the specified location is given a specified color, overwriting the old color.

Input: Upon entry:

x-coordinate (0-319) of the point is in SI
y-coordinate (0-199) of the point is in DI
color (0-3) is in DX

Output: Just to the screen.

Registers Used: No registers are modified. SI, DI, and DX are used for input.

Segments Referenced: Upon entry ES must point to the video RAM at B8000h and DS must point to a data segment containing the following look-up table of rotated color masks:

```
table   dw      0003Fh, 0403Fh, 0803Fh, 0C03Fh
        dw      000CFh, 010CFh, 020CFh, 030CFh
        dw      000F3h, 004F3h, 008F3h, 00CF3h
        dw      000FCh, 001FCh, 002FCh, 003FCh
```

Routines Called: None

Special Notes: No bounds checking is performed. The user must make sure that the coordinates and the color are in their proper ranges.

```
ROUTINE TO PLOT A POINT ON MEDIUM RES COLOR SCREEN

etpt    proc    far

        push    bx              ; save registers
        push    si
        push    ax

multiply y-coord by bytes per row and adjust for even/odd lines
        mov     ax,di           ; get y-coord into low part
        mov     ah,al           ;  and into high part
```

```
        and     ax,Ø1FEh        ; mask off unwanted parts
        sal     ax,1            ; times 4
        sal     ax,1            ; times 8
        sal     ax,1            ; times 16
        mov     bx,ax           ; goes into address
        and     bh,7            ; without adjustment
        sal     ax,1            ; times 32
        sal     ax,1            ; times 64
        add     bx,ax           ; address gets y-coord times 8Ø
;
; add x-coord to address
        mov     ax,si           ; get x-coordinate
        sar     ax,1            ; divide
        sar     ax,1            ; by 4
        add     bx,ax           ; here is the address
;
; compute the rotated mask and color
        and     si,3            ; just pixel position into the index
        sal     si,1            ; index times 2
        sal     si,1            ; index times 4
        add     si,dx           ; 4*pixel position + color
        sal     si,1            ; 8*pixel position + 2*color
        mov     ax,ctable[si]   ; look up rotated color and mask
;
; insert the color into the video byte
        and     al,es:[bx]      ; get old byte & remove old pixel
        or      al,ah           ; insert new color
        mov     es:[bx],al      ; put the byte back
;
        pop     ax              ; restore registers
        pop     si
        pop     bx
        ret
;
setpt   endp
```

XORPT

XOR a Point onto the Medium Resolution Color Screen

Function: This routine plots a point on the medium resolution screen using the "exclusive or" operation. The pixel at the specified location is colored with a color obtained by "exclusive oring" its original color with a specified color. This function is useful for making cursors.

Input: Upon entry:

> x-coordinate (0-319) of the point is in SI
> y-coordinate (0-199) of the point is in DI
> color mask (0-3) for xor is in DX

Output: Just to the screen.

Registers Used: No registers are modified. SI, DI, and DX are used for input.

Segments Referenced: Upon entry ES must point to the video RAM at B8000h and DS must point to a data segment containing the following look-up table for rotated color masks:

```
able   dw      0003Fh, 0403Fh, 0803Fh, 0C03Fh
       dw      000CFh, 010CFh, 020CFh, 030CFh
       dw      000F3h, 004F3h, 008F3h, 00CF3h
       dw      000FCh, 001FCh, 002FCh, 003FCh
```

Routines Called: None

Special Notes: No bounds checking is performed. The user must make sure that the coordinates and the color are in their proper ranges.

```
ROUTINE TO XOR A POINT ONTO MEDIUM RES COLOR SCREEN

rpt    proc    far

       push    bx              ; save registers
       push    si
       push    ax

multiply y-coord by bytes per row and adjust for even/odd lines
       mov     ax,di           ; get y-coord into low part
```

```
        mov     ah,al           ;  and into high part
        and     ax,Ø1FEh        ; mask off unwanted parts
        sal     ax,1            ; times 4
        sal     ax,1            ; times 8
        sal     ax,1            ; times 16
        mov     bx,ax           ; goes into address
        and     bh,7            ; without adjustment
        sal     ax,1            ; times 32
        sal     ax,1            ; times 64
        add     bx,ax           ; address gets y-coord times 8Ø
;
; add x-coord to address
        mov     ax,si           ; get x-coordinate
        sar     ax,1            ; divide
        sar     ax,1            ; by 4
        add     bx,ax           ; here is the address
;
; compute the mask for color and use it
        and     si,3            ; just the bit count into the index
        sal     si,1            ; index times 2
        sal     si,1            ; index times 4
        add     si,dx           ; 4*pixel position + color
        sal     si,1            ; 8*pixel position + 2*color
        mov     ax,ctable[si]   ; look up the masks
        xor     es:[bx],ah      ; xor the byte with the color
;
        pop     ax              ; restore registers
        pop     si
        pop     bx
        ret
;
xorpt   endp
```

LOCATE

Locate a Point on the Medium Resolution Color Screen

Function: This routine returns the color of a point on the medium resolution screen. The color is returned in AL.

Input: Upon entry:

x-coordinate (0-319) of the point is in SI
y-coordinate (0-199) of the point is in DI

Output: Upon exit AL contains the color (0-3) of the pixel at the specified location.

Registers Used: Only AX is modified. SI and DI are used for input and AL is used for output.

Segments Referenced: Upon entry ES must point to the video RAM at B8000h.

Routines Called: None

Special Notes: No bounds checking is performed. The user must make sure that the coordinates are in their proper ranges.

```
ROUTINE TO RETURN COLOR OF A POINT ON MEDIUM RES COLOR SCREEN

ocate   proc    far

        push    bx              ; save registers
        push    cx

multiply y-coord by bytes per row and adjust for even/odd lines
        mov     ax, di          ; get y-coord into low part
        mov     ah, al          ;  and into high part
        and     ax, 01FEh       ; mask off unwanted parts
        sal     ax, 1           ; times 4
        sal     ax, 1           ; times 8
        sal     ax, 1           ; times 16
        mov     bx, ax          ; goes into address
        and     bh, 7           ; without adjustment
        sal     ax, 1           ; times 32
        sal     ax, 1           ; times 64
        add     bx, ax          ; address gets times 64 + times 16
```

```
;
; add x-coord to address
        mov     ax,si           ; get x-coordinate
        sar     ax,1            ; divide
        sar     ax,1            ; by 4
        add     bx,ax           ; here is the address
;
; compute the position of the pixel in the byte
        mov     cx,si           ; use x-coordinate to determine count
        and     cx,3            ; just the bit count
        inc     cx              ; plus one
        sal     cx,1            ; 2 bits per pixel
;
; get the byte and rotate into place
        mov     al,es:[bx]      ; get old byte
        rol     al,cl           ; rotate left this many times
        and     ax,3            ; just the pixel color
;
        pop     cx              ; restore the registers
        pop     bx
        ret
;
locate  endp
```

SETBOX

Fill a Rectangular Box with Color

Function: This routine fills a rectangular box in the color graphics screen with a given color.

Input: Upon entry:

x-coordinate of upper left corner is in x1
y-coordinate of upper left corner is in y1
x-coordinate of lower right corner is in x2
y-coordinate of lower right corner is in y2
color of the rectangle is in bits 0 and 1 of color

Output: Just to the screen.

Registers Used: No registers are modified.

Segments Referenced: Upon entry ES must point to the video RAM at B8000h and DS must point to the following look-up table for color masks:

```
table  dw       0FFC0h, 0FFF0h, 0FFFCh, 0FFFFh
       dw       03FC0h, 03FF0h, 03FFCh, 03FFFh
       dw       00FC0h, 00FF0h, 00FFCh, 00FFFh
       dw       003C0h, 003F0h, 003FCh, 003FFh
```

Routines Called: None

Special Notes: No bounds checking is performed. The coordinates must be in range and in order. That is, the following must be true:

0 <= x1 <= x2 <= 319
0 <= y1 <= y2 <= 199

```
ROUTINE TO FILL A RECTANGULAR BOX

etbox  proc    far

       push    si              ; save registers
       push    di
       push    dx
       push    bx
```

```
                push    cx
                push    ax
;
; determine byte position for start
;
; get y contribution
                mov     ax,y1           ; get starting y-coordinate
                mov     ah,al           ; replicate for odd/even bank
                and     ax,1FEh         ; just one bit gets moved
                sal     ax,1            ; times 4
                sal     ax,1            ; times 8
                sal     ax,1            ; times 16
                mov     di,ax           ; address gets 16 times y-coordinate
                and     di,7FFh         ; not the odd/even bit
                sal     ax,1            ; times 32
                sal     ax,1            ; times 64
                add     di,ax           ; address gets 8Ø times y-coordinate
;
; add in x contribution
                mov     ax,x1           ; get x-coordinate
                sar     ax,1            ; divide
                sar     ax,1            ;  by 4
                add     di,ax           ; beginning offset
;
; count for outer loop
                mov     cx,y2           ; ending y-coordinate
                sub     cx,y1           ; minus starting y-coordinate
                inc     cx              ; plus one
;
; count for inner loop
                mov     si,x2           ; ending x-coordinate
                sar     si,1            ; divide
                sar     si,1            ;  by 4
                mov     ax,x1           ; starting x-coordinate
                sar     ax,1            ; divide
                sar     ax,1            ;  by 4
                sub     si,ax           ; take the difference
;
; get the color
                mov     bx,color        ; get the color
                and     bx,3            ; just between Ø and 3
                mov     dl,cbytes[bx]   ; look up color pattern
;
; determine mask for start and ending bytes
                mov     bx,x1           ; starting byte
                and     bx,3            ; just the pixel position
                sal     bx,1            ; times 2
                sal     bx,1            ; times 4
                mov     ax,x2           ; ending byte
```

```
        and     ax,3            ; just the pixel position
        add     bx,ax           ; 4*starting+ending
        sal     bx,1            ; 8*starting+2*ending
        mov     bx,xtable[bx]   ; look up the masks

; set up masked color bytes
        mov     dh,dl           ; color for left bytes
        mov     ah,dl           ; color for middle bytes
        and     dx,bx           ; mask left and right color bytes

        cld                     ; forward

sboxloop:
        push    cx              ; save count of outer loop
        push    di              ; save initial byte position

        mov     cx,si           ; count for inner loop

; check for only one byte
        mov     al,bh           ; get the mask
        jcxz    sboxloop2       ; if ending byte coincides

; color leftmost byte of the scan line
        not     al              ; reverse the mask for clearing
        and     al,es:[di]      ; get byte from memory and clear pixels
        or      al,dh           ; put color in place
        stosb                   ; put byte in place

; check for just two bytes
        dec     cx              ; count the byte
        jcxz    sboxloop1       ; done?

; color middle bytes of the scan line
        mov     al,ah           ; color for middle bytes
        rep     stosb           ; put middle bytes in place

; handle rightmost byte of the scan line

; come here if two or more bytes
sboxloop1:
        mov     al,ØFFh         ; set full mask

; in any case come here to adjust the masks
sboxloop2:
        and     al,bl           ; bring in right part of mask
        and     dl,al           ; clear left part of color if needed
```

```
;
; color the byte
        not     al              ; reverse the mask for clearing
        and     al,es:[di]      ; get byte from memory and clear pixels
        or      al,dl           ; put pixels in the byte
        stosb                   ; put byte back into video RAM
;
; compute next scan line
        pop     di              ; restore address of left side of box
        test    di,2000h        ; odd or even line?
        jz      sboxloop3       ; skip if even
        add     di,80           ; add 80 bytes per line
sboxloop3:
        xor     di,2000h        ; changes banks in any case
        pop     cx              ; restore count for outer loop
        loop    sboxloop        ; next scan line
;
        pop     ax              ; restore registers
        pop     cx
        pop     bx
        pop     dx
        pop     di
        pop     si
        ret
;
setbox  endp
```

XORBOX

XOR Fill a Rectangular Box with Color

Function: This routine fills a rectangular box in the color graphics screen with a given color using the "exclusive or" operation. Each pixel in the rectangle is colored with a color obtained by "exclusive oring" its original color with a specified color. This function is useful for making cursors.

Input: Upon entry:

    x-coordinate of upper left corner is in x1
    y-coordinate of upper left corner is in y1
    x-coordinate of lower right corner is in x2
    y-coordinate of lower right corner is in y2
    color of the rectangle is in bits 0 and 1 of color

Output: Just to the screen.

Registers Used: No registers are modified.

Segments Referenced: Upon entry ES must point to the video RAM at B8000h and DS must point to the following look up table for color masks:

```
able  dw      0FFC0h, 0FFF0h, 0FFFCh, 0FFFFh
      dw      03FC0h, 03FF0h, 03FFCh, 03FFFh
      dw      00FC0h, 00FF0h, 00FFCh, 00FFFh
      dw      003C0h, 003F0h, 003FCh, 003FFh
```

Routines Called: None

Special Notes: No bounds checking is performed. The coordinates must be in range and in order. That is, the following must be true:

    0 <= x1 <= x2 <= 319
    0 <= y1 <= y2 <= 199

```
ROUTINE TO XOR A RECTANGULAR BOX

rbox  proc    far

      push    si              ; save registers
```

```
        push    di
        push    dx
        push    bx
        push    cx
        push    ax
;
; determine byte position for start
;
; get y contribution
        mov     ax,y1           ; get starting y-coordinate
        mov     ah,al           ; replicate for odd/even bank
        and     ax,1FEh         ; just one bit gets moved
        sal     ax,1            ; times 4
        sal     ax,1            ; times 8
        sal     ax,1            ; times 16
        mov     di,ax           ; address gets 16 times y-coordinate
        and     di,7FFh         ; not the odd/even bit
        sal     ax,1            ; times 32
        sal     ax,1            ; times 64
        add     di,ax           ; address gets 80 times y-coordinate
;
; add in x contribution
        mov     ax,x1           ; get x-coordinate
        sar     ax,1            ; divide
        sar     ax,1            ;  by 4
        add     di,ax           ; beginning offset
;
; count for outer loop
        mov     cx,y2           ; ending y-coordinate
        sub     cx,y1           ; minus starting y-coordinate
        inc     cx              ; plus one
;
; count for inner loop
        mov     si,x2           ; ending x-coordinate
        sar     si,1            ; divide
        sar     si,1            ;  by 4
        mov     ax,x1           ; starting x-coordinate
        sar     ax,1            ; divide
        sar     ax,1            ;  by 4
        sub     si,ax           ; take the difference
;
; get the color
        mov     bx,color        ; get the color
        and     bx,3            ; just between 0 and 3
        mov     dl,cbytes[bx]   ; look up color pattern
;
; determine mask for start and ending bytes
        mov     bx,x1           ; starting byte
        and     bx,3            ; just the pixel position
```

```
        sal    bx,1              ; times 2
        sal    bx,1              ; times 4
        mov    ax,x2             ; ending byte
        and    ax,3              ; just the pixel position
        add    bx,ax             ; 4*starting+ending
        sal    bx,1              ; 8*starting+2*ending
        mov    bx,xtable[bx]     ; look up the masks

;set up masked color bytes
        mov    dh,dl             ; color for left bytes
        mov    ah,dl             ; color for middle bytes
        and    dx,bx             ; mask left and right color bytes

        cld                      ; forward direction

;xloop:
        push   cx                ; save count for outer loop
        push   di                ; save address of leftmost byte

        mov    cx,si             ; count for inner loop

;check if only one byte in a scan line
        mov    al,bh             ; get the mask
        jcxz   xboxloop3         ; ending byte coincides

;xor the leftmost byte
        xor    es:[di],dh        ; xor color into memory
        inc    di                ; next byte
        dec    cx                ; count it
        jcxz   xboxloop2         ; done?

;xor the middle bytes
;xloop1:
        xor    es:[di],ah        ; xor color byte into memory
        inc    di                ; next byte
        loop   xboxloop1         ; loop to get all the middle

;handle the rightmost byte

;come here if two or more bytes
;xloop2:
        mov    al,ØFFh           ; set full mask

;in any case come here to adjust
;xloop3:
        and    al,bl             ; bring in right part
        and    dl,al             ; mask the color if needed
```

```
;
; xor the rightmost byte
        xor     es:[di],dl      ; xor byte into memory
        inc     di              ; next byte
;

        pop     di              ; restore the leftmost address
        test    di,2000h        ; odd or even scan line?
        jz      xboxloop4       ; skip if even
        add     di,80           ; add 80 if odd
xboxloop4:
        xor     di,2000h        ; switch banks in any case
        pop     cx              ; restore count of outer loop
        loop    xboxloop        ; loop for next scan line
;

        pop     ax              ; restore registers
        pop     cx
        pop     bx
        pop     dx
        pop     di
        pop     si
        ret
;
xorbox  endp
```

econd Level Functions

This section contains the next level of graphics routines. These routines have to perform their tasks quickly and so should be written in assembly language. However, they do not access the screen directly. Instead, they call upon the routines in the previous section to make any input or output to the screen.

SETLINE

Draw a Line

Function: This routine draws a line from (x1,y1) to (x2,y2) in the specified color. It uses Bresenham's algorithm.

Input: Upon entry:

x1 contains x-coordinate of starting point
y1 contains y-coordinate of starting point
x2 contains x-coordinate of ending point
y2 contains y-coordinate of ending point
color contains the color of the line

Output: Just to the screen.

Registers Used: No registers are modified.

Segments Referenced: Upon entry ES must point to the video RAM at B8000h and DS must point to a data segment used by the point-plotting routine (see SETPT or XORPT above).

Routines Called: SETPT

Special Notes: No bounds checking is performed. The user must make sure that the coordinates and the color are in their proper ranges. That is, x1 and x2 must be between 0 and 319, y1 and y2 must be between 0 and 199, and color must be between 0 and 3.

```
ROUTINE TO DRAW LINE

tline proc    far
      push    bx              ; save registers
      push    cx
```

```
        push    dx
        push    si
        push    di
        push    ax
;
; set up x and y updates
        mov     si,1            ; start with positive 1 for x update
        mov     di,1            ; start with positive 1 for y update
;
; find |y2-y1|
        mov     dx,y2           ; get y2
        sub     dx,y1           ; subtract y1
        jge     storey          ; skip if y2-y1 is nonnegative
        neg     di              ; move in negative y direction
        neg     dx              ; absolute value of y2-y1
storey:
        mov     deldy,di        ; store y update for diagonal moves
;
; find |x2-x1|
        mov     cx,x2           ; get x2
        sub     cx,x1           ; subtract x1
        jge     storex          ; skip if x2-x1 is nonnegative
        neg     si              ; move in negative x direction
        neg     cx              ; absolute value of x2-x1
storex:
        mov     deldx,si        ; store x update for diagonal moves
;
; sort |y2-y1| and |x2-x1|
        cmp     cx,dx           ; compare dels with delp
        jge     setdiag         ; skip if straight moves in x direction
        mov     si,0            ; if straight=vertical: kill x update
        xchg    cx,dx           ;    and exchange differences
        jmp     storedelsxy
;
setdiag:
        mov     di,0            ; if straight=horizontal: kill y update

; store dels, delp, delsx, and delsy
storedelsxy:
        mov     dels,cx         ; change in straight direction
        mov     delp,dx         ; change in perpendicular to straight
        mov     delsx,si        ; x update in straight direction
        mov     delsy,di        ; y update in straight direction
;
; get initial values for x and y
        mov     si,x1           ; x-coordinate
        mov     di,y1           ; y-coordinate
```

```
; compute initial value and increments for error function
        mov     ax, delp
        sal     ax, 1           ; 2*delp
        mov     delse, ax       ; change if straight move

        sub     ax, cx          ; 2*delp - dels
        mov     bx, ax          ; initial value

        sub     ax, cx          ; 2*delp - 2*dels
        mov     delde, ax       ; change if diagonal move

; adjust count
        inc     cx

; set the color
        mov     dx, color       ; get the color

; main loop structure
lineloop:
        call    setpt           ; plot the point
        cmp     bx, Ø           ; determine straight or diagonal move
        jge     diagonal

; case for straight move
straight:
        add     si, delsx       ; update x
        add     di, delsy       ; update y
        add     bx, delse       ; update error term
        loop    lineloop        ; next point
        jmp     lineexit

; case for diagonal move
diagonal:
        add     si, deldx       ; update x
        add     di, deldy       ; update y
        add     bx, delde       ; update error term
        loop    lineloop        ; next point

lineexit:
        pop     ax              ; restore registers
        pop     di
        pop     si
        pop     dx
        pop     cx
        pop     bx
        ret

setline endp
```

SCHAR

Plot a Stroke Character

Function: This routine plots a stroke character. It uses a stroke character table in which each character is stored as a series of strokes. The user must create this stroke character table according to specific rules. Each stroke is stored as three bytes. The first byte contains a code as follows:

1Ah = end of strokes
'U' = pen Up, move to new current position, but don't draw
'D' = pen Down, draw a stroke from old to new current position

The second byte contains the local x-coordinate of the new current position, and the third byte contains the local y-coordinate of the new current position. These local coordinates are relative to the upper left corner of the character cell. At the beginning of the stroke table is a table of addresses for the locations of the strokes for each of the characters.

Input: Upon entry:

ASCII code character is in AL
x-coordinate of upper left corner of character cell is in x0
y-coordinate of upper left corner of character cell is in y0
horizontal magnitude is in xmagn
vertical magnitude is in ymagn
color of the character is in color

Output: Just to the screen.

Registers Used: No registers are modified.

Segments Referenced: Upon entry ES must point to the video RAM at B8000h and DS must point to the data segment used by the point and line-drawing routines. This data segment must also contain the table of stroke characters.

Routines Called: SETLINE

Special Notes: No bounds checking is performed. Unpredictable results happen if the horizontal or vertical magnitude is too large. A string of raster characters can be printed using the GMESSOUT routine below.

ROUTINE TO PLOT A STROKE CHARACTER

```
char    proc    far

        push    si              ; save registers
        push    cx
        push    ax

        cbw                     ; make the ASCII code into 16-bit
        sal     ax,1            ; times 2
        mov     si,ax           ; into the index
        mov     si,ptable[si]   ; look up the particular character
        mov     ax,xØ           ; x-coordinate of upper left corner
        mov     x2,ax
        mov     ax,yØ           ; y-coordinate of upper left corner
        mov     y2,ax

; run through the strokes
newstroke:
        lodsb                   ; get the code byte
        cmp     al,1ah          ; end of strokes?
        jz      scharexit
        mov     dl,al           ; save code

; update x-coordinate of current position
        mov     ax,x2           ; old x-coordinate
        mov     x1,ax           ; gets pushed back
        lodsb                   ; new x-coordinate
        mov     cl,xmagn        ; times xmagn
        mul     cl              ; multiply
        add     ax,xØ           ; add to upper left corner
        mov     x2,ax           ; and put into current position

; update y-coordinate of current position
        mov     ax,y2           ; old y-coordinate
        mov     y1,ax           ; gets pushed back
        lodsb                   ; new y-coordinate
        mov     cl,ymagn        ; times ymagn
        mul     cl              ; multiply
        add     ax,yØ           ; add to upper left corner
        mov     y2,ax           ; put in current position

        cmp     dl,'U'          ; pen up?
        je      newstroke       ; skip if so

        call    setline         ; draw the stroke

        jmp     newstroke       ; next stroke
```

```
;
scharexit:
        pop     ax              ; restore registers
        pop     cx
        pop     si
        ret
;
schar   endp
```

RCHAR

Plot a Raster Character

Function:　　This routine plots a raster character. It uses the raster character table in the IBM BIOS ROM. Only ASCII codes 0 through 127 are supported.

Input:　　Upon entry:

ASCII code character is in AL
x-coordinate of upper left corner of character cell is in x0
y-coordinate of upper left corner of character cell is in y0
horizontal magnitude is in xmagn
vertical magnitude is in ymagn
color of the character is in color

Output:　　Just to the screen.

Registers Used:　　No registers are modified.

Segments Referenced:　　Upon entry ES must point to the video RAM at B8000h and DS must point to the data segment used by the box-fill routine.

Routines Called:　　SETBOX

Special Notes:　　No bounds checking is performed. Unpredictable results happen if the horizontal or vertical magnitude is too large. A string of raster characters can be printed using the GMESSOUT routine below.

```
ROUTINE TO PLOT A RASTER CHARACTER

char    proc    far

        push    si              ; save registers
        push    dx
        push    cx
        push    ax

look up pattern for character
        cbw                     ; convert from byte to word
        sal     ax,1            ; times 2
        sal     ax,1            ; times 4
```

```
          sal     ax,1             ; times 8
          add     ax,ØFA6Eh+7      ; character table + pattern end
          mov     si,ax            ; here is the offset
;
          mov     dx,ds            ; save old DS
          mov     ax,ØFØØØh        ; point DS to ROM segment
          mov     ds,ax            ; here is the data segment
;
; store the pattern on the stack
          mov     cx,8             ; for a count of eight bytes
          std                      ; backward direction
rchar1:
          lodsb                    ; load
          push    ax               ; push onto stack
          loop    rchar1
;
          mov     ds,dx            ; restore data segment
;
; get the starting point
          mov     ax,xØ            ; get x-coordinate
          mov     x1,ax
          mov     ax,yØ            ; get y-coordinate
          mov     y1,ax
;
          mov     cx,8             ; for a count of 8 rows
rchar2:
          pop     dx               ; get the next row
          push    cx               ; save the count
;
          mov     al,ymagn         ; vertical sizing
          cbw
          dec     ax               ; one less
          add     ax,y1            ; add to new dot position
          mov     y2,ax
;
          mov     cx,8             ; for a count of 8 dots
rchar3:
          push    cx               ; save the count
;
          mov     al,xmagn         ; horizontal sizing
          cbw
          dec     ax               ; one less
          add     ax,x1            ; add to new dot position
          mov     x2,ax
;
          test    dl,8Øh           ; check the dot
          jz      rchar4           ; skip it if zero
```

```
        call    setbox          ; plot it if one
char4:
        mov     ax,x2           ; next column
        inc     ax              ; one over from end of box
        mov     x1,ax           ; into next dot position
        rol     dl,1            ; next dot from pattern
        pop     cx              ; restore count of dots
        loop    rchar3          ; loop for next dot

        mov     ax,xØ           ; restore to first column
        mov     x1,ax           ; beginning of row
        mov     ax,y2           ; next row
        inc     ax              ; one down from end of box
        mov     y1,ax           ; into next row position
        pop     cx              ; restore count of rows
        loop    rchar2          ; loop for next row

        pop     ax              ; restore registers
        pop     cx
        pop     dx
        pop     si
        ret

char    endp
```

GMESSOUT

Print a String on the Graphics Screen

Function: This routine prints a message on the graphics screen, using the SCHAR or RCHAR routines above. The message terminates in a zero.

Input: Upon entry:

address of message is in SI
x-coordinate of upper left corner of string is in xmess
y-coordinate of upper left corner of string is in ymess
horizontal magnitude of characters is in xmagn
vertical magnitude of characters is in ymagn
color of characters is in color
choice of fonts (0 = stroke, 1 = raster) is in font

Output: Just to the screen.

Registers Used: No registers are modified.

Segments Referenced: Upon entry ES must point to the video RAM at B8000h and DS must point to the data segment used by the point-plotting, box-filling, line-drawing, and stroke character routines.

Routines Called: RCHAR and SCHAR

Special Notes: No bounds checking is performed. Unpredictable results happen if the horizontal or vertical magnitude is too large.

```
; ROUTINE TO PRINT A MESSAGE ON THE GRAPHICS SCREEN
;
gmessout        proc    far
;
; get (x,y) location of message on the screen
        mov     ax,xmess        ; get x-coordinate on screen
        mov     xØ,ax           ; for first character
        mov     ax,ymess        ; get y-coordinate on screen
        mov     yØ,ax           ; for first character
        cld                     ; go in forward direction
```

```
; main loop through characters of the message
gmessloop:
        cld                         ; forward direction
        lodsb                       ; get the ASCII code
        cmp     al,Ø                ; end of string?
        je      gmessexit

; check for fonts
font0:
        cmp     font,Ø              ; use font Ø?
        jne     font1
        call    schar               ; stroke characters

font1:
        cmp     font,1              ; use font 1?
        jne     nextchar
        call    rchar               ; raster characters

nextchar:
        mov     al,8                ; character cell width
        mov     cl,xmagn            ; times horizontal magnitude
        mul     cl                  ; multiply
        add     xØ,ax               ; add to location of previous char

        jmp     gmessloop           ; loop for next character

gmessexit:
        ret
gmessout        endp
```

Fill an Area on the Screen with Color

Function: This routine fills an area on the graphics screen with a specified color. It starts "painting" at a "seed" position, filling a region bounded by a "boundary" color. It uses an algorithm, developed over the past few years in the computer graphics literature. The algorithm has been implemented by a number of my students. In particular, Joe Vierra implemented it in 8088 assembly code for another graphics device. This is a modified version of Joe's program. The registers have been changed to protect the innocent.

Input: Upon entry:

   x-coordinate of seed is in SI
   y-coordinate of seed is in DI
   paint color is in the low byte of color
   boundary color is in the high byte of color

Output: Just to the screen.

Registers Used: No registers are modified.

Segments Referenced: Upon entry ES must point to the video RAM at B8000h and DS must point to the data segment used by the point-plotting and locate routine.

Routines Called: SETPT and LOCATE

Special Notes: The region must be completely surrounded by a boundary drawn in the boundary color. Any paint color in the region can obstruct the filling process, acting just like a boundary. This algorithm uses its own stack. If the region is too complex this stack will overflow. There is no check for such a stack overflow, but a check can easily be added.

```
; ROUTINE TO FILL AN AREA
;
; preliminary push and pop procedures
;
; pushpaint pushes x- and y-coordinates on paint stack
```

```
ushpaint         proc    near
        dec     bp                  ; BP is the paint stack pointer
        dec     bp                  ; and gets decremented first
        mov     [bp],si             ; push x
        dec     bp
        dec     bp
        mov     [bp],di             ; push y
        ret                         ; return

ushpaint         endp

; poppaint pops x- and y-coordinates on paint stack
oppaint          proc    near
        mov     di,[bp]             ; pop y
        inc     bp                  ; increment stack after
        inc     bp
        mov     si,[bp]             ; pop x
        inc     bp
        inc     bp
        ret
oppaint          endp

aint    proc    far

; initialize paint color
        mov     dx,color

; initialize paint stack
        lea     bp,paintstack       ; BP is set to top of stack
        call    pushpaint           ; push seed onto stack

; main loop for painting
aint1:
        lea     ax,paintstack       ; stack empty?
        cmp     bp,ax
        jne     paint2              ; continue if not
        jmp     endpaint            ; exit if not

; get the next place to paint
aint2:
        call    poppaint            ; pop the next place to paint
        call    locate              ; color is returned in AL
        cmp     al,dl               ; is it filled?
        je      paint1
        cmp     al,dh               ; is it boundary?
        je      paint1
        cmp     di,∅                ; top of screen?
        jl      paint1
        cmp     di,199              ; bottom of screen?
        jg      paint1
```

```
;
; move right until boundary is reached
paint3:
        inc     si              ; x <-- x + 1
        call    locate          ; look right
        dec     si              ; restore x
;
        cmp     al,dl           ; is it filled?
        je      paint4
        cmp     al,dh           ; is it boundary color?
        je      paint4
        cmp     si,319          ; at right screen boundary?
        je      paint4
        inc     si              ; x <-- x + 1
        jmp     paint3
;
; push above and below
paint4:
        dec     di              ; y <-- y - 1
        call    locate          ; check above
        mov     bh,al           ; save above state
        cmp     al,dl           ; is it filled?
        je      paint5
        cmp     al,dh           ; is it boundary color?
        je      paint5
        call    pushpaint       ; push above
paint5:
        inc     di              ; restore y
        inc     di              ; y <-- y + 1
        call    locate          ; check below
        mov     bl,al           ; save below state
        cmp     al,dl           ; is it filled?
        je      paint6
        cmp     al,dh           ; is it boundary color?
        je      paint6
        call    pushpaint       ; push below
;
paint6:
        dec     di              ; restore y
;
; anchor the end point of the scan line
        mov     x2,si           ; store x-coord of end of scan line
        mov     y2,di           ; store y-coord of end of scan line
;
; plot as we scan left, checking above and below
;
paint7:
; check above
        dec     di              ; y <-- y - 1
        call    locate          ; check above
```

```
        cmp     al,dl           ; is it filled?
        je      paint9
        cmp     al,dh           ; is it boundary color?
        je      paint9

        cmp     bh,dl           ; last above filled?
        je      paint8
        cmp     bh,dh           ; was it boundary color?
        je      paint8
        jmp     paint9

paint8:
        call    pushpaint       ; push above if new place to paint
paint9:
        mov     bh,al           ; update last above

        inc     di              ; restore y

; check below
        inc     di              ; y <-- y + 1
        call    locate          ; check below
        cmp     al,dl           ; is it filled?
        je      paint11
        cmp     al,dh           ; is it boundary color?
        je      paint11

        cmp     bl,dl           ; last below filled?
        je      paint1Ø
        cmp     bl,dh           ; was it boundary color?
        je      paint1Ø
        jmp     paint11

paint1Ø:
        call    pushpaint       ; push below if new place to paint
paint11:
        dec     di              ; restore y
        mov     bl,al           ; update last below

; move left
        dec     si              ; x <-- x - 1
        jl      paint12         ; stop the scan if too far left
        call    locate          ; check the point
        cmp     al,dl           ; hit filled yet?
        je      paint12         ;   if so next scan line
        cmp     al,dh           ; hit boundary yet?
        je      paint12         ;   if so next scan line
        jmp     paint7          ; continue painting the scan line
```

```
paint12:
        inc     si              ; restore x
        mov     x1,si           ; store x-coordinate of start
        mov     y1,di           ; store y-coordinate of start
        call    setbox          ; plot the scan line
        jmp     paint1          ; next place to paint
;
endpaint:
        ret
;
paint   endp
```

Sound

The routines in this chapter use the speaker on the IBM PC to produce various sounds and musical tones. There is even a routine to play music.

Sound is an important component in making computers behave in a more friendly manner. Right now sound is more important in games than in other areas of computing. However, once computers are able to accurately and efficiently understand spoken commands, sound will most likely be one of the primary methods of input and output.

The first few routines, TONEINIT, TONESET, TONEON, and TONEOFF, are primitives; that is, they access the speaker and its associated timer directly. All other routines call these routines to produce any sound.

The speaker is connected to the output of the timer which produces a square wave whose frequency can be set using the TONESET routine. TONESET assumes that the timer has been properly initialized. This is done during normal boot-up of the IBM PC. We have included a routine TONEINIT which also initializes the timer.

The frequency of the square wave from the timer is determined by the following formula:

$$f = F/n$$

where f is the frequency of the square wave, F is 1,193,182, and n is a 16-bit integer that is input to the routine. The quantity F is the frequency of a clock signal which runs the timer. This frequency is exactly one third the frequency of the NTSC subcarrier used for color encoding by the Color/Graphics Adapter. F is derived by hardware from a main clock signal that runs at 14,317,800 cycles per second and supplies the timing for most of the computer.

TONEON and TONEOFF give the programmer control over whether or not the square wave reaches the speaker, thus turning on and off the sound. There are actually two bits involved, one to control the connection between the clock signal and the timer, and one to control the connection between the timer and the speaker. Both routines switch both connections simultaneously. We found it unnecessary to control the bits independently.

The routine DELAY provides timing for the duration of musical tones in milliseconds. The routine FREQ uses the formula:

$$n = F/f$$

to compute the input parameter for TONESET from a given frequency. Using this just before the TONESET routine allows a programmer to work directly with frequencies rather than clock cycles of the 1,193,182 hertz clock.

Next comes the routine TONE that uses the other routines to produce tones of a given frequency and a given duration. The frequency is input as a 16-bit integer and the duration is in milliseconds using the DELAY routine.

The next four routines are built around the idea of white noise. The first routine SCALE converts numbers between 0 and 1 to numbers between x1 and x2, where x1 and x2 are any specified 16-bit integers. This is used in conjunction with RANDOM which produces pseudo-random numbers between 0 and 1. In the routine WHITE these pseudo-random numbers are scaled into frequencies and fed to the timer to generate white noise. The routine GUN then shows how to shape white noise into a machine gun sound.

The routines GLISSANDO and RED provide more special effects. GLISSANDO makes a tone which smoothly slides from one frequency to another, and RED shows how to shape glissandos into red alert sirens.

The routines in the last section are music routines. PITCH simply converts the pitch number to the value required by TONESET to set the frequency. PLAY plays music from a "playlist" of notes. VICTORY and HORN are programs containing playlists which call PLAY to play specific melodies.

Sound Primitives

The routines TONEINIT, TONESET, TONEON, and TONEOFF are sound primitives. They access the speaker and its associated timer directly. All the other sound-producing routines in this chapter call these routines to set frequency or turn the sound on and off.

TONEINIT

Initialize Speaker Timer

Function: This routine initializes the portion of the 8253 timer chip used by the speaker system. In particular, it sets up channel 2 of this timer as a square wave generator. This routine does not select the frequency nor turn on the tone. Use TONESET to select the frequency, TONEON to turn the tone on, and TONEOFF to turn it off.

Input: None

Output: Only to the timer 2 of the speaker circuit.

Registers Used: No registers are modified.

Segments Referenced: None

Routines Called: None

Special Notes: None

```
; ROUTINE TO SET TONE
;
; define control bit field parameters for the timer chip
sc      =       2               ; use counter 2
rl      =       3               ; mode to load period one byte at a time
mode    =       3               ; square wave generator
bcd     =       Ø               ; not bcd, use binary values
;
; form control word
cnword  =       sc*4Øh + rl*1Øh + mode*2 + bcd
;
toneinit        proc    far
;
        push    ax              ; save registers
```

```
;send control word to 8253 timer chip
        mov     al,cnword       ; select the above control word
        out     43h,al          ; send it out the control port

        pop     ax              ; restore registers
        ret

einit           endp
```

TONESET

Set the Tone on the Speaker

Function: This routine selects the frequency of the square wave tone to the speaker. The input to this routine is a 16-bit integer n which determines the frequency f according to the following formula:

$$f = F/n$$

where F is 1,193,182, the frequency of a clock signal which feeds the timer. The value n is the number of cycles of the clock signal per cycle of the resulting square wave. This routine does not actually turn on the tone. Use TONEON to turn the tone on and TONEOFF to turn it off. This routine assumes that the speaker timer has already been properly initialized. This happens during normal boot-up of the computer, or you can use TONEINIT to initialize this timer.

Input: Upon entry the 16-bit integer n is in the CX register.

Output: Only to the timer 2.

Registers Used: No registers are modified.

Segments Referenced: None

Routines Called: None

Special Notes: None

```
; ROUTINE TO SELECT TONE
;
toneset proc    far
;
        push    ax              ; save registers

; load the time period into the timer
        mov     al,cl           ; lower byte
        out     42h,al          ; out to timer
        mov     al,ch           ; upper byte
        out     42h,al          ; out to timer
;
        pop     ax              ; restore registers
        ret
;
toneset endp
```

TONEON

Turn on Tone

Function: Turns on the timer and speaker to produce a tone. The frequency of the tone must have already been selected on the timer. You can use TONESET to set the frequency of the tone.

Input: None

Output: To the timer and speaker only.

Registers Used: No registers are modified.

Segments Referenced: None

Routines Called: None

Special Notes: None

```
;  ROUTINE TO TURN ON TONE
;
toneon  proc    far
;
        push    ax              ; save registers
;
; turn speaker and timer on
        in      al,61h          ; get contents of system port B
        or      al,3            ; turn speaker and timer on
        out     61h,al          ; send out new values to port B
;
        pop     ax              ; restore registers
        ret
;
toneon  endp
```

TONEOFF

Turn off Tone

Function: This routine turns off the timer and speaker.

Input: None

Output: To the timer and speaker only.

Registers Used: No registers are modified.

Segments Referenced: None

Routines Called: None

Special Notes: None

```
; ROUTINE TO TURN TONE OFF
;
toneoff proc    far
;
        push    ax              ; save registers
;
; turn off timer 2 and speaker
        in      al,61h          ; get port B again
        and     al,11111100b    ; turn off timer and speaker
        out     61h,al          ; now do it
;
        pop     ax              ; restore registers
        ret
;
toneoff endp
```

Making Tones

The first routine in this section, DELAY, provides a time delay for specifying the duration of a sound (or for any other purpose). The second routine, FREQ, converts a frequency to the number needed by TONESET to specify the pitch of a note. The final routine in this section, TONE, puts together a number of other routines to produce a tone of a given frequency and duration.

DELAY

Delay for Specified Number of Milliseconds

Function: Delays a specified number of milliseconds.

Input: Upon input CX contains the number of milliseconds to delay.

Output: None

Registers Used: No registers are modified.

Segments Referenced: None

Routines Called: None

Special Notes: None

```
; ROUTINE TO DELAY SPECIFIED NUMBER OF MILLISECONDS
delay    proc    far

         push    cx              ; save registers

delay1:
         push    cx              ; save counter
         mov     cx,260          ; timing constant
delay2:
         loop    delay2          ; small loop
         pop     cx              ; restore counter
         loop    delay1          ; loop to count milliseconds

         pop     cx              ; restore registers
         ret

delay    endp
```

FREQ

Conversion from Frequency to Period

Function: This routine converts from frequency to the number required by TONESET to set the frequency. The routine performs the following formula:

$$n = F/f$$

where f is the frequency input to this routine, n is the number output by this routine, and F is 1,193,182. In other words this routine divides the specified frequency f into the 1,193,182 hertz clock frequency that drives the timer. Use this routine just before TONESET.

Input: Upon entry the frequency is in CX.

Output: Upon exit F/f is in CX.

Registers Used: Only CX is modified.

Segments Referenced: None

Routines Called: None

Special Notes: None

```
; ROUTINE TO CONVERT FROM FREQUENCY TO PERIOD
;
freq    proc    far
;
        push    dx              ; save registers
        push    ax
;
        mov     dx, 12h         ; upper part of numerator
        mov     ax, 34DEh       ; lower part of numerator
        div     cx              ; divide by frequency
        mov     cx, ax          ; the quotient is the output
;
        pop     ax              ; restore registers
        pop     dx
        ret
;
freq    endp
```

TONE

Make a Tone

Function: This routine makes a tone of a given frequency and given length.

Input: Upon entry the frequency is in CX and the length in number of milliseconds is in DX.

Output: To the speaker and timer only.

Registers Used: No registers are modified.

Segments Referenced: The data segment must contain the variable COUNT.

Routines Called: TONESET, TONEON, TONEOFF, DELAY

Special Notes: The speaker timer must already have been properly initialized. This should happen during boot-up.

```
ROUTINE TO MAKE TONE

one     proc    far

        push    dx              ; save registers
        push    cx
        push    ax

compute the frequency and set up the tone
        call    freq            ; convert the frequency
        call    toneset         ; set up the tone

turn on the tone
        call    toneon          ; turn it on

wait for proper delay
        mov     cx,dx           ; get delay length
        call    delay

turn off the tone
        call    toneoff         ; turn it off
```

```
;
        pop     ax              ; restore registers
        pop     cx
        pop     dx
        ret
;
tone    endp
```

Special Effects

The routines in this section demonstrate how to use the IBM PC sound system to produce such special effects as machine gun sounds and red alert sirens. The first is based upon the idea of white noise and the second upon the idea of glissandos (sliding frequencies). Both of these concepts are explicitly developed in their own routines, WHITE and GLISSANDO. There are two helper routines, SCALE and RANDOM, that are useful in other situations besides sound generation.

SCALE

Linear Scaling

Function: This routine performs a linear scaling, converting a fixed point number between 0 and 1 to an integer between X1 and X2, where X1 and X2 are 16-bit integers.

Input: Upon entry CX has a binary fixed point number between 0 and 1. The binary point is to the left of the leftmost bit. X1 and X2 are variables stored in memory.

Output: Upon exit CX contains the 16-bit integer result.

Registers Used: Only CX is modified.

Segments Referenced: The data segment must contain the variables X1 and X2.

Routines Called: None

Special Notes: None

```
ROUTINE TO SCALE LINEARLY

scale   proc    far

        push    dx              ; save registers
        push    ax

compute width
        mov     ax,x2           ; get x2
        sub     ax,x1           ; subtract x1
```

```
;
; multiply width by input parameter
        mul     cx              ; multiply
        mov     cx,dx           ; move top part of quotient into CX
;
; add lower limit
        add     cx,x1           ; add x1
;
        pop     ax              ; restore registers
        pop     dx
        ret
;
scale   endp
```

RANDOM

Pseudo-Random Number Generator

Function: This routine generates pseudo-random numbers between 0 and 1. The numbers are stored in 16-bit binary fixed point notation with the binary point on the extreme left.

Input: Upon entry the variable SEED contains a seed value.

Output: Upon exit the seed is updated and the CX register contains a pseudo-random number.

Registers Used: Only CX is modified.

Segments Referenced: Upon entry the data segment contains the variable SEED.

Routines Called: None

Special Notes: None

```
random  proc    far

        mov     cx, seed        ; get the seed
        add     cx, 9248h       ; add random pattern
        ror     cx, 1           ; rotate
        ror     cx, 1           ; three
        ror     cx, 1           ; times
        mov     seed, cx        ; put it back

        ret

random  endp
```

WHITE

White Noise

Function: This routine makes white noise of a given frequency range.

Input: Upon entry the lower limit to the frequency is in BX, the upper limit to the frequency is in CX, and a measure of the duration of the noise is in DX. This last value is just the number of times that the frequency is changed while the routine runs.

Output: To the speaker and timer only.

Registers Used: No registers are modified.

Segments Referenced: The data segment must contain the variables x1 and x2.

Routines Called: TONESET, TONEON, TONEOFF

Special Notes: The speaker timer must already have been initialized. This should happen during boot-up or TONEINIT may be used.

```
; ROUTINE TO MAKE WHITE NOISE
;
white    proc    far
;
         push    dx              ; save registers
         push    cx
         push    ax
;
         mov     x1,bx           ; lower limit of frequencies
         mov     x2,cx           ; upper limit of frequencies
;
         mov     seed,Ø          ; initialize seed
         call    freq            ; convert the frequency
         call    toneset         ; set the frequency
         call    toneon          ; turn the tone on
;
         mov     cx,dx           ; get number of times
white1:
         push    cx              ; save count
         call    random          ; generate a random number (Ø-1)
         call    scale           ; scale between x1 and x2
         call    freq            ; convert the frequency
```

```
        call    toneset         ; set the tone
        pop     cx              ; restore count
        loop    white1

turn off the tone
        call    toneoff         ; turn it off

        pop     ax              ; restore registers
        pop     cx
        pop     dx
        ret

hite    endp
```

GUN

Machine Gun

Function: This routine makes a machine gun noise.

Input: None

Output: To the speaker and timer only.

Registers Used: No registers are modified.

Segments Referenced: The data segment must contain the variables x1 and x2.

Routines Called: WHITE, DELAY

Special Notes: The speaker timer must already have been initialized. This happens during boot-up.

```
; ROUTINE TO MAKE MACHINE GUN SOUND
;
gun     proc    far
;
        push    dx              ; save registers
        push    cx
        push    bx
;
        mov     cx, 1Ø
gun1:
        push    cx              ; save the count
        mov     bx, 256         ; lower limit of frequencies
        mov     cx, 4Ø96        ; upper limit of frequencies
        mov     dx, 256         ; controls length
        call    white           ; use white noise for gun
        mov     cx, 5Ø          ; 4ØØ millisecond
        call    delay           ; delay
        pop     cx              ; restore the count
        loop    gun1
;
        pop     bx              ; restore registers
        pop     cx
        pop     dx
        ret
;
gun     endp
```

GLISSANDO

Make a Glissando

Function: This routine makes a glissando, that is, a sound which slides from one frequency to another. The rate of change can be controlled.

Input: Upon entry the beginning frequency is in BX, the ending frequency is in CX, and the control parameter for the rate increase is in DX. Increasing the value in DX slows down the rate of change.

Output: To the speaker and timer only.

Registers Used: No registers are modified.

Segments Referenced: The data segment must contain the variables x1 and x2.

Routines Called: TONESET, TONEON, TONEOFF, DELAY

Special Notes: The speaker timer must already have been initialized. If necessary, use TONEINIT to initialize the speaker timer before calling this routine.

```
ROUTINE TO MAKE GLISSANDO

lissando        proc     far

        push     si              ; save registers
        push     dx
        push     cx
        push     bx
        push     ax

        mov      x1,bx           ; lower limit of frequencies
        mov      x2,cx           ; upper limit of frequencies

        call     toneon          ; turn on tone

set up the loop parameters
        mov      si,1            ; increment for loop
        cmp      bx,cx           ; up or down?
        jle      gliss1          ; skip if up
```

```
;
        neg     si              ; decrement freq in the loop
;
gliss1:
        mov     cx,bx           ; get the frequency
        call    freq            ; convert to clock cycles
        call    toneset         ; set the tone
        mov     cx,dx           ; delay parameter
gliss2:
        loop    gliss2

        cmp     bx,x2           ; check if done
        je      gliss3          ; exit if so
        add     bx,si           ; update the frequency
;
        jmp     gliss1
;
;
gliss3:
; turn off the tone
        call    toneoff         ; turn it off
;
        pop     ax              ; restore registers
        pop     bx
        pop     cx
        pop     dx
        pop     si
        ret
;
glissando       endp
```

Red Alert

Function: This routine makes a red alert sound consisting of ten rapid upward glissandos.

Input: None

Output: To the speaker and timer only.

Registers Used: No registers are modified.

Segments Referenced: The data segment must contain the variables x1 and x2.

Routines Called: GLISSANDO

Special Notes: The speaker timer must already have been initialized. This should happen during boot-up.

```
ROUTINE TO MAKE RED ALERT

red     proc    far

        push    dx              ; save registers
        push    cx
        push    bx

        mov     cx,10           ; ten glissandos
red1:
        push    cx              ; save the counter
        mov     bx,256          ; starting frequency
        mov     cx,4096         ; ending frequency
        mov     dx,1            ; delay factor
        call    glissando       ; now make the glissando
        pop     cx              ; restore the loop count
        loop    red1

        pop     bx              ; restore registers
        pop     cx
        pop     dx
        ret

red     endp
```

Play Music

The routines in this section show how to make the IBM PC play music. PITCH converts pitch numbers of a multioctave chromatic scale to the proper value to set the frequency with TONESET. PLAY reads a binary "play" file to play a tune. VICTORY and HORN are two complete programs that call upon the PLAY routine to perform their own binary "play" files. VICTORY plays a bugle call often heard at race tracks and HORN plays the first few bars of a horn concerto by Richard Strauss.

Convert from Pitch Number

Function: This routine converts from pitch number to the value required by TONESET to set the frequency. The pitch numbers refer to an extended chromatic scale. The notes of this scale are numbered from 0 to 95 with 12 notes per octave. 0 corresponds to a C at 16.35 hertz.

Input: Upon entry the pitch number of the note is in AL.

Output: Upon exit the DX register contains the proper value for TONESET.

Registers Used: No registers are modified.

Segments Referenced: The data segment must contain the following pitch table:

notes	dw	4186	; C
	dw	4435	; C sharp/D flat
	dw	4699	; D
	dw	4978	; D sharp/E flat
	dw	5274	; E
	dw	5588	; F
	dw	5920	; F sharp/G flat
	dw	6272	; G
	dw	6645	; G sharp/A flat
	dw	7040	; A
	dw	7459	; A sharp/B flat
	dw	7902	; B

Routines Called: FREQ

Special Notes: None

ROUTINE TO DETERMINE PITCH

```
tch     proc    far

        push    cx              ; save registers
        push    bx
        push    ax

        mov     ah,Ø            ; extend pitch number to 16 bits
        mov     cl,12           ; divisor of 12
        div     cl              ; divide

        mov     dl,al           ; quotient determines the octave
        mov     al,ah           ; remainder is the pitch within
        cbw                     ; 16-bit needed for look up
        sal     ax,1            ; 2 bytes per item
        mov     bx,ax           ; into BX
        mov     cx,notes[bx]    ; look it up
        call    freq            ; convert the frequency

        xchg    cx,dx           ; octave in cl, period in DX
        neg     cl              ; 8 - octave = shift count
        add     cl,8
        sal     dx,cl

        pop     ax              ; restore registers
        pop     bx
        pop     cx
        ret

tch     endp
```

PLAY

Play Music

Function: This is a program which plays music. It reads a binary "play" list which contains instructions to make the tune. This list consists of a series of music instructions. In this particular implementation, there are four instructions: Tempo, Note, Rest, and End. The syntax for each is as follows:

Tempo Command:
  first byte   = ASCII "T"
  second byte = tempo in whole notes per minute

Note Command:
  first byte   = ASCII "N"
  second byte = pitch number (integer 0-95)
  third byte   = length (8-bit binary fixed point – scale 1)
  fourth byte = style (8-bit binary fixed point – scale 0)

Rest Command:
  first byte   = ASCII "R"
  second byte = length (8-bit binary fixed point – scale 1)

End Command:
  first byte   = ASCII "X"

The scaling is as follows: scale 0 has the binary point to the left of the leftmost digit and scale 1 has the binary point to the right of the leftmost bit.

Input: Upon entry the address of the "play" list is in DS:SI.

Output: To the speaker and timer only.

Registers Used: No registers are modified.

Segments Referenced: The data segment contains the "play" list and the variables WHOLE, ACOUNT, and RCOUNT.

Routines Called: PITCH, TONEOFF, DELAY

Special Notes: None

; ROUTINE TO PLAY MUSIC

```
play    proc    far

        push    ds              ; save registers
        push    si
        push    dx
        push    cx
        push    bx
        push    ax
```

; command pointer is in SI

; set the default tempo
```
        mov     whole,2000      ; 2000 milliseconds for a whole note

        cld                     ; forward direction
```

; main loop starts here
```
play1:
```

; get the command code and go through the cases
```
play2:
        lodsb                   ; get the byte
```

; End command
```
        cmp     al,'X'          ; End command?
        jne     play3
        jmp     playexit
```

; Tempo command
```
play3:
        cmp     al,'T'          ; Tempo command?
        jne     play4

        lodsb                   ; get the tempo
        mov     cl,al           ; set in CX
        mov     ch,0
        mov     ax,60000        ; number of milliseconds per minute
        mov     dx,0            ; upper part is cleared
        div     cx              ; divide into time
        mov     whole,ax        ; number of milliseconds per whole note
        jmp     play1           ; back for more
```

; Note command
```
play4:
        cmp     al,'N'          ; Pitch command?
        jne     play5
```

```
        ;
                lodsb                       ; get the pitch
                call    pitch               ; convert
                mov     cx,dx               ; and move result into CX
                call    toneset             ; set the frequency
                call    toneon              ; turn on the tone
        ;
                mov     cx,whole            ; number of milliseconds per whole note
        ;
                lodsb                       ; get the duration
                mov     ah,al               ; set up duration as multiplier
                mov     al,Ø
                sal     cx,1                ; scale factor 1
                mul     cx                  ; multiply
        ;
                mov     cx,dx               ; total count for the note
        ;
                lodsb                       ; get style
                mov     ah,al               ; set up style as multiplier
                mov     al,Ø
                mul     cx                  ; multiply by style
        ;
                mov     acount,dx           ; store count for note
                sub     cx,dx               ; count for rest
                mov     rcount,cx           ; store count for rest
        ;
                mov     cx,acount           ; audible part of note
                call    delay               ; delay
                call    toneoff             ; turn off the tone
                mov     cx,rcount           ; inaudible part of note
                call    delay               ; delay
        ;
                jmp     play1               ; back for more
        ;
        ; Rest command
        play5:
                cmp     al,'R'              ; Rest command?
                jne     play6
        ;
                mov     cx,whole            ; number of milliseconds per whole note
        ;
                lodsb                       ; get the duration
                mov     ah,al               ; set up duration as multiplier
                mov     al,Ø
                sal     cx,1                ; scale factor of 1
                mul     cx                  ; multiply
        ;
                mov     cx,dx               ; total count
                call    delay               ; delay
```

```
        jmp     play1           ; back for more

; Anything else ends it
play6:
        jmp     playexit        ; stay on exit command

playexit:
        pop     ax              ; restore registers
        pop     bx
        pop     cx
        pop     dx
        pop     si
        pop     ds
        ret

play    endp
```

VICTORY

Play a Victory Bugle Call

Function: This program plays a victory bugle call.

Input: The "play" list is in the data segment included in the program.

Output: To the speaker only.

Registers Used: This is an EXE file which uses registers as needed.

Segments Referenced: The relevant part of the data segment is included.

Routines Called: PLAY

Special Notes: None

```
;---------------------- external reference ------------------------+
; EXTERNAL REFERENCES
        extrn   play:far
;---------------------- stack segment -----------------------------+
stacks  segment stack
        db      20 dup('stack   ')
stacks  ends
;---------------------- data segment ------------------------------+
datas   segment public
;
; play list for "victory" bugle call
victory db      'T',60
        db      'N',55, 32,128
        db      'N',60, 32,128
        db      'N',64, 32,128
        db      'N',67, 48,228
        db      'N',67, 16,228
        db      'N',67, 32,228
        db      'N',64, 48,228
        db      'N',64, 16,228
        db      'N',64, 32,228
        db      'N',60, 32,128
        db      'N',64, 32,128
```

```
        db      'N',6Ø, 32,128
        db      'N',55, 96,24Ø
        db      'X'

tas    ends
--------------------- code segment -----------------------------+
des    segment

        assume  cs: codes, ss: stacks, ds: datas

in     proc    far

art:
        push    ds              ; set return address segment
        mov     ax,Ø            ;  and offset
        push    ax

        mov     ax, datas       ; get data segment
        mov     ds, ax          ; into DS

        lea     si, victory     ; point to the play list
        call    play            ; play the tune

        ret                     ; return to DOS

ain    endp

odes   ends
        end     start
```

HORN

Play Opening of Strauss Horn Concerto

Function: This program plays the opening bars of a French horn concerto by Richard Strauss (Concerto No. 1 in E flat).

Input: The "play" list is in the data segment included in the program.

Output: To the speaker only.

Registers Used: This is an EXE file which uses registers as needed.

Segments Referenced: The relevant part of the data segment is included.

Routines Called: PLAY

Special Notes: None

```
;---------------------- external reference ------------------------+
; EXTERNAL REFERENCES
        extrn   play:far
;---------------------- stack segment -----------------------------+
stacks  segment stack
        db      20 dup('stack   ')
stacks  ends
;---------------------- data segment ------------------------------+
datas   segment public
;
; play list for horn concerto
horn    db      'T',28
        db      'N',58, 24,192
        db      'N',62,  8,192
;
        db      'N',65, 96,192
        db      'N',62, 24,192
        db      'N',67,  8,192
;
        db      'N',65, 32,192
        db      'N',62, 24,192
        db      'N',58,  8,192
        db      'N',53, 32,192
        db      'N',58, 24,192
        db      'N',62,  8,192
```

```
        db      'N',6Ø,  32,192
        db      'N',58,  24,192
        db      'N',53,   8,192
        db      'N',5Ø,  32,192
        db      'N',46,  24,192
        db      'N',55,   8,192

        db      'N',53,  64,192
        db      'N',41,  64,192
        db      'X'

tas     ends
---------------------- code segment --------------------------------+
des     segment

        assume  cs:codes,ss:stacks,ds:datas

in      proc    far

art:
        push    ds              ; set return address segment
        mov     ax,Ø            ;   and offset
        push    ax

        mov     ax,datas        ; get data segment
        mov     ds,ax           ; into DS

        lea     si,horn         ; point to the play list
        call    play            ; play the tune

        ret                     ; return to DOS

in      endp

des     ends
        end     start
```

9

Strings

*S*tring manipulation is an important part of computing which is useful in such areas as text editing and data base management. The routines in this chapter are fundamental to both of these application areas.

The first two routines (LOWERCASE and UPPERCASE) convert characters within a string from upper- to lowercase and from lower- to uppercase.

The next two routines (STRSEARCH and STRINSERT) require two input strings. STRSEARCH searches for a copy of one string in another, and STRINSERT inserts a copy of one string within another.

Next are two routines (LEXSEARCH and LEXINSERT) that require a string and a *list* of strings as input. LEXSEARCH searches for the proper place to insert a string in a lexigraphically ordered list of strings, and LEXINSERT inserts a string in the proper place in a lexigraphically ordered list of strings. Lexigraphical order is another name for alphabetical order. However, you should understand that for these routines the individual characters are ordered according to their ASCII code. For example, all uppercase letters precede any lowercase letter. You can easily change the routines so that all lowercase letters are converted to uppercase before being used in comparisons for lexigraphic ordering of the words.

LEXINSERT is built upon earlier routines in that it calls LEXSEARCH to find the proper spot and then calls STRINSERT to make the insertion.

The last three routines (COMPARE, SWITCH, and BSORT) work with string arrays. COMPARE is used to compare two strings of equal length. It enables you to compare two different entries of the same string array. SWITCH is used to switch two strings of the same length, for example, two different entries of the same string array. Both of these routines are needed by BSORT, which performs a bubble sort of a string array. Although bubble sort is definitely not one of the fastest methods of sorting, it is extremely easy to program, as you can see from our BSORT routine. Because this routine is written in assembly language it runs fast in spite of the slowness of the method.

In these routines we have taken advantage of the 8088 string instructions. Notice how easy they make string scanning and comparing; the COMPARE routine has only one instruction besides the PUSHes and POPs to save the registers.

LOWERCASE

Convert to Lower Case

Function: This routine converts the characters in a string to lower case.

Input: Upon entry DS:BX points to a string. The first two bytes in the string form a 16-bit integer which specifies its length. The remaining bytes contain the characters of the string.

Output: Upon exit all alphabetical characters of the string are lower case.

Registers Used: No registers are modified.

Segments Referenced: Upon entry the data segment must contain the string.

Routines Called: None

Special Notes: None

```
; ROUTINE TO CONVERT STRING TO LOWER CASE
;
lowercase       proc    far
;
        push    bx              ; save registers
        push    cx
        push    ax
;
; get the length
        mov     cx,[bx]         ; first two bytes contain the length
        inc     bx              ; point to beginning of text
        inc     bx
;
; loop through the bytes of the string
lowercase1:
        mov     al,[bx]         ; get the character
        cmp     al,'A'          ; below the upper case characters?
        jb      lowercase2      ; skip if so
        cmp     al,'Z'          ; above the upper case characters?
        ja      lowercase2      ; skip if so
;
        or      al,20h          ; OR bit 5 into the byte
```

```
owercase2:
        mov     [bx],al         ; store the character
        inc     bx              ; point to next character
        loop    lowercase1

        pop     ax              ; restore registers
        pop     cx
        pop     bx
        ret

owercase         endp
```

UPPERCASE

Convert to Upper Case

Function:　This routine converts the characters in a string to upper case.

Input:　Upon entry DS:BX points to a string. The first two bytes in the string form a 16-bit integer which specifies its length. The remaining bytes contain the characters of the string.

Output:　Upon exit all alphabetical characters of the string are upper case.

Registers Used:　No registers are modified.

Segments Referenced:　Upon entry the data segment must contain the string.

Routines Called:　None

Special Notes:　None

```
; ROUTINE TO CONVERT STRING TO UPPER CASE
;
uppercase       proc    far
;
        push    bx              ; save registers
        push    cx
        push    ax
;
; get the length
        mov     cx, [bx]        ; first two bytes contain the length
        inc     bx              ; point to beginning of text
        inc     bx
;
; loop through the bytes of the string
uppercase1:
        mov     al, [bx]        ; get the character
        cmp     al, 'a'         ; below the lower case characters?
        jb      uppercase2      ; skip if so
        cmp     al, 'z'         ; above the lower case characters?
        ja      uppercase2      ; skip if so
;
        and     al, 5Fh         ; mask out bit number 5
```

```
percase2:
        mov     [bx],al         ; store the character
        inc     bx              ; point to next character
        loop    uppercase1

        pop     ax              ; restore registers
        pop     cx
        pop     bx
        ret

percase         endp
```

STRSEARCH

Search for One String Within Another

Function: This routine searches for a copy of a source string within a destination string.

Input: Upon entry DS:BX points to a source string and ES:DX points to a destination string. Each string begins with a 16-bit integer which specifies its length.

Output: Upon exit AL contains a return flag (0 = not found, 0FFh = found), and if the search was successful DX contains the location of the first byte of the match in the destination.

Registers Used: Only AX and DX are modified. They are used for output.

Segments Referenced: Upon entry the data segment must contain the source string and the extra segment must contain the destination string.

Routines Called: None

Special Notes: None

```
; ROUTINE TO SEARCH FOR ONE STRING WITHIN ANOTHER
;
strsearch       proc    far
;
        push    si              ; save registers
        push    di
        push    cx
;
; get length of destination and point to first byte
        mov     si,dx           ; use source index
        lodsw                   ; get the length of destination
        mov     cx,ax           ; use the length as a count
        mov     dx,si           ; text begins here
;
strsearch1:
; point indices to beginning of source and destination
        mov     si,bx           ; load source index
        mov     di,dx           ; load destination index
```

```
scan for match
        mov     al, [si+2]          ; get the first character
        cld                         ; forward direction
        repnz   scasb               ; scan for match
        jcxz    strsearch2          ; quit if found no match

got a match of first characters - now check the entire string
        mov     dx, di              ; save current destination loc
        dec     di                  ; beginning of word
        lodsw                       ; get length of source
        xchg    cx, ax              ; use source count and save dest count
        repz    cmpsb               ; compare the two strings
        jcxz    strsearch3          ; it's a match if no more source

continue the scan
        xchg    cx, ax              ; use destination count
        jmp     strsearch1          ; back for more scanning of dest

no match is possible
trsearch2:
        mov     al, Ø               ; unsuccessful outcome
        jmp     strsearchexit

found a match
trsearch3:
        dec     dx                  ; point to beginning of match
        mov     al, ØFFh            ; successful match
        jmp     strsearchexit

strsearchexit:
        pop     cx                  ; restore registers
        pop     di
        pop     si
        ret

strsearch        endp
```

STRINSERT

Insert One String in Another

Function: This routine inserts a source string in a specified place in a destination string. See Figure 9-1.

Input: Upon entry DS:BX points to the source string, ES:BP points to the destination string, and ES:DX points to the spot in the destination where the source is to be placed. Each string begins with a 16-bit integer which specifies its length.

Output: Upon exit the destination string has the source string inserted in the proper place. The length of the destination is increased accordingly.

Registers Used: No registers are modified.

Segments Referenced: Upon entry the data segment must contain the source string and the extra segment must contain the destination string.

Routines Called: None

Special Notes: None

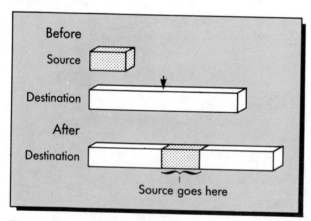

Figure 9-1.   String insertion

```
; ROUTINE TO INSERT ONE STRING WITHIN ANOTHER
;
;
; addressing equates
essorc    equ      es:[si]        ; equate for source in extra seg
dsdest    equ      byte ptr[di]   ; equate for usual destination
```

```
trinsert          proc     far

          push     si                ; save registers
          push     di
          push     cx
          push     ax

find current end of destination string
          mov      si,bp             ; start of string
          add      si,es:[si]        ; point to next to last byte
          inc      si                ; adjust for length information

find new end of destination string and update length
          mov      di,si             ; get old end of destination
          mov      ax,[bx]           ; get length of source
          add      di,ax             ; new end of destination
          add      es:[bp],ax        ; new length of destination

move tail of destination string out of the way
          mov      cx,si             ; SI - DX + 1 is the count
          sub      cx,dx
          inc      cx
          std                        ; backward direction
ep        movs     dsdest,essorc     ; move the tail

move source string into place
          mov      di,dx             ; destination of move
          mov      si,bx             ; source of move
          cld                        ; forward direction
          lodsw                      ; length of source
          mov      cx,ax             ; the count
          rep      movsb             ; make the string move

trinsertexit:
          pop      ax                ; restore registers
          pop      cx
          pop      di
          pop      si
          ret

trinsert          endp
```

LEXSEARCH

Search a Lexigraphically Ordered List

Function: This routine searches a lexigraphically (alphabetically) ordered list of word strings for the proper place to insert a new word.

Input: Upon entry DS:BX points to a source word string, ES:BP points to the ordered list of words. The source word string begins with a 16-bit integer which is its length and then continues with the bytes of the string. The last byte must be a carriage return symbol (ASCII 13). The destination list of words begins with a 16-bit integer which specifies its length in character bytes and continues with words which consist of ASCII characters. The words are separated by carriage return symbols (ASCII 13). See Figure 9-2.

Output: Upon exit AL contains a return flag (0 = not found, 0FFh = found). If the search was successful ES:DX contains the location of the proper place to insert the new word. If the word was already present then ES:DX points to the location of this word in the destination.

Registers Used: Only AX and DX are modified because they are used for output.

Segments Referenced: Upon entry the data segment must contain the source string and the extra segment must contain the destination word list.

Routines Called: None

Special Notes: None

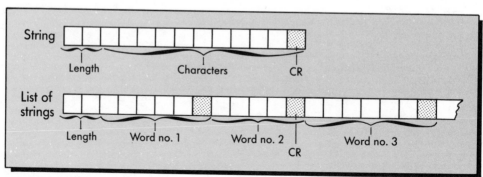

Figure 9-2. Data structures for LEXSEARCH

ROUTINE TO SEARCH FOR A WORD IN AN ORDERED LIST OF WORDS

```
xsearch          proc     far

        push     si                  ; save registers
        push     di
        push     cx

point to beginning of list and get its length
        mov      di,bp               ; beginning of list
        mov      cx,[di]             ; get length
        inc      di
        inc      di

compare source word with words in the list

xsearch1:

        mov      dx,di               ; save beginning of dest word

forward direction
        cld                          ; forward direction

point to beginning of source
        mov      si,bx               ; point to beginning of source
        inc      si
        inc      si

compare source word with a word of the list
xsearch2:

check for end of list
        jcxz     lexsearch5          ; end of list - insert it

set up carriage return as character for scanning
        mov      al,13               ; scan for carriage return

check for end of source word
        cmp      [si],al             ; source byte = carriage return?
        je       lexsearch4          ; end of source word found

check for end of destination word
        cmp      es:[di],al          ; dest byte = carriage return?
        je       lexsearch3          ; no match - go to next word

compare character by character
        dec      cx
        cmpsb                        ; check for match
        je       lexsearch2          ; matched - check next character
        jb       lexsearch5          ; too high - this is the place
```

```
;
; scan for next carriage return
lexsearch3:
        repnz   scasb           ; scan until carriage return
        jmp     lexsearch1      ; next word
;
; end of source word was found
lexsearch4:
        cmp     [di],al         ; dest character = carriage return?
        je      lexsearch6      ; end of destination word?
;
; found a spot to insert the word
lexsearch5:
        mov     al,ØFFh         ; success
        jmp     lexsearchexit
;
; word is already present
lexsearch6:
        mov     al,ØØh          ; already there
        jmp     lexsearchexit
;
lexsearchexit:
        pop     cx              ; restore registers
        pop     di
        pop     si
        ret
;
lexsearch        endp
```

LEXINSERT

Lexigraphically Insert

Function: This routine inserts a word string in the proper place in a lexigraphically (alphabetically) ordered list of word strings. If the word is already present, no insertion takes place.

Input: Upon entry DS:BX points to a source word string, ES:BP points to the ordered list of words. The source word string begins with a 16-bit integer which specifies its length. The last byte must be a carriage return symbol (ASCII 13). The destination list of words begins with a 16-bit integer which specifies its length and continues with words which consist of ASCII characters. The words are separated by carriage return symbols (ASCII 13). See Figure 9-2.

Output: Upon exit the list has the string inserted in the proper place.

Registers Used: No registers are modified.

Segments Referenced: Upon entry the data segment and the extra segment must be equal and must contain the source string and the destination word list.

Routines Called: LEXSEARCH, STRINSERT

Special Notes: None

```
ROUTINE TO INSERT A WORD IN AN ORDERED LIST OF WORDS

lexinsert       proc    far

    push    ax              ; save registers

    call    lexsearch       ; search for match
    cmp     al,Ø            ; already there?
    je      lexinsertexit   ; skip if so
    call    strinsert       ; insert the new word

lexinsertexit:
    pop     ax              ; restore registers
    ret

lexinsert       endp
```

COMPARE

Compare Two Strings

Function: This routine compares two strings of the same length.

Input: Upon entry DS:SI points to one string (the source) and DS:DI points to a second string (the destination). Both strings have lengths given by CX.

Output: Upon exit the flags specify the relation of the source to the destination:

    l = source string is less than the destination string
    e = source string is equal to the destination string
    g = source string is greater than the destination string

Registers Used: Only AX is modified.

Segments Referenced: Upon entry the data segment contains the source string and the extra segment contains the destination string.

Routines Called: None

Special Notes: None

```
; ROUTINE TO COMPARE TWO STRINGS
;
compare proc    far
;
        push    si              ; save registers
        push    di
        push    cx
;
        repz    cmpsb           ; one compare does it!
;
        pop     cx              ; restore registers
        pop     di
        pop     si
        ret
;
compare endp
```

SWITCH

Switch Two Strings

Function: This routine switches two strings.

Input: Upon entry DS:SI points to one string (the source) and ES:DI points to a second string (the destination). Both strings have lengths given by CX.

Output: Upon exit the strings are switched.

Registers Used: No registers are modified.

Segments Referenced: Upon entry the data segment contains the source string and the extra segment contains the destination string.

Routines Called: None

Special Notes: None

```
ROUTINE TO SWITCH TWO STRINGS

switch  proc    far

        push    si              ; save registers
        push    di
        push    cx
        push    ax

        cld                     ; forward direction
switch1:
        mov     al,[di]         ; get byte from destination
        movsb                   ; move from source to destination
        mov     es:[si-1],al    ; put byte in source
        loop    switch1         ; loop back for more

        pop     ax              ; restore registers
        pop     cx
        pop     di
        pop     si
        ret

switch  endp
```

BSORT

Bubble Sort a String Array

Function: This routine sorts a string array using bubble sort.

Input: Upon entry DS:SI points to a string array, CX contains the number of entries in the array, and DX contains the size of each entry.

Output: Upon exit the array is sorted.

Registers Used: No registers are modified.

Segments Referenced: Upon entry the data segment and the extra segment must be equal and must contain the string array.

Routines Called: COMPARE, SWITCH

Special Notes: None

```
; ROUTINE TO SORT A STRING ARRAY
;
bsort     proc    far
;
          push    si              ; save registers
          push    di
          push    cx
          push    ax
;
; adjust count for one less than number of items
          dec     cx              ; adjust the count
;
; outer loop - for SI = 1 to N-1
bsort1:
          push    cx              ; save the count
          mov     di,si           ; destination points to source
;
; inner loop - for DI = SI+1 to N
bsort2:
          push    cx              ; save the count
          add     di,dx           ; point to next destination
          mov     cx,dx           ; entry length
          call    compare         ; compare the strings
          jle     bsort3          ; skip if source <= dest
          call    switch          ; switch if not
```

```
bsort3:
        pop     cx              ; restore the count
        loop    bsort2

        add     si,dx           ; point to next source
        pop     cx              ; restore the count
        loop    bsort1
bsortexit:
        pop     ax              ; restore registers
        pop     cx
        pop     di
        pop     si
        ret

bsort   endp
```

10

File Manipulation

*T*his chapter contains routines which are designed to assist with the manipulation of files. Included are routines to transfer files from a serial communications line to disk and routines to "filter" files within the system.

The routines are designed to use the new "file handle" DOS calls available starting with PC DOS version 2. These new calls greatly simplify assembly language programming of disk files; instead of dealing with multibyte file control blocks, the assembly language programmer deals with single 16-bit integers which uniquely specify each file. This frees the assembly language programmer from many details better left to the operating system, allowing the programmer to work at a higher level.

Version 2 of PC DOS also has *filters*, a Unix-like feature which, among other things, allows an assembly language programmer to develop and thoroughly test text processing routines in the friendly environment of the keyboard and screen and then, once the worst bugs are out, use these same routines, unmodified, to manipulate disk files.

The first routine, EMESSOUT, is designed to report errors to the user. It prints out various error messages on the screen, given their error codes. We have extended the error codes and the corresponding error messages beyond those included in the Error Return Table in the IBM DOS 2 Operating System Manual. We have added six more codes: 0, 14, 19, 20, 21, and 22. Code 0 (a "ready" message) is added to slightly simplify the message routine; code 14 (which we have assigned to "Message not in use") was missing from the original table; and codes 19 through 22 were necessitated by error conditions generated by the routines in this chapter.

Actually, not all conditions listed in our table are errors. For example, "end of file" is often a desirable outcome even though it is exceptional. Hence, the more general term *exception* is used. In this spirit we have called this routine *Exception Message Output* and the table it references *Exception Message Table*.

The second routine GETSPEC is useful for getting file specifiers for creating or opening files using "file handles". When you type in a transient command with parameters such as file specifiers, these parameters are loaded into an area of memory called the "unformatted parameter area". GETSPEC retrieves these parameters from this area and places them wherever you specify.

The next few routines, CREATEFILE, CLOSEFILE, WRITEFILE, and READFILE, are general purpose file-handling routines using "file handles".

The next five routines INITCBUFF, PUTCBUFF, INCBUFF, FLUSHIT, and OUTCBUFF handle input and output for a circular buffer. A circular buffer is a software device for handling a stream of bytes which is coming in at a different rate than it is going out. The circular buffer consists of a linear stretch of memory whose end is wrapped around to its beginning via software (see Figure 10-1), together with handshaking protocols to control the flow in and out of this linear memory. This is particularly useful for interfacing disks to communications lines in order to receive files. In this case the byte streams are often quite large and the input and output rates often differ by several orders of magnitude.

There are four variables and three constants associated with our particular circular buffer. The variables are CBUFF and GAUGE (held in memory), an input pointer held in the DI register, and an output pointer held in the SI register. CBUFF is the base address of the buffer and GAUGE is the number of items currently in the buffer. As items are added to the buffer, they are placed where the input pointer points and the input pointer is incremented to point to the next available location. As items are removed from the buffer, they are taken from where the output buffer points and the output buffer is incremented to point to the next item to be output.

The constants for our circular buffer are BUFFSIZE, NEAREMPTY, and NEARFULL. BUFFSIZE is the total number of bytes (or items, in a more general context) allotted to the buffer; NEAREMPTY and NEARFULL are limits on how few or many items should be in the buffer at any one time. NEARFULL is the most important because it helps to prevent the buffer from overflowing. When the buffer is nearly full (as measured by NEARFULL) the software calls upon a routine to cut off the flow of any more input. Since it sometimes takes a while for the flow to stop, especially if input is coming from an external device, there

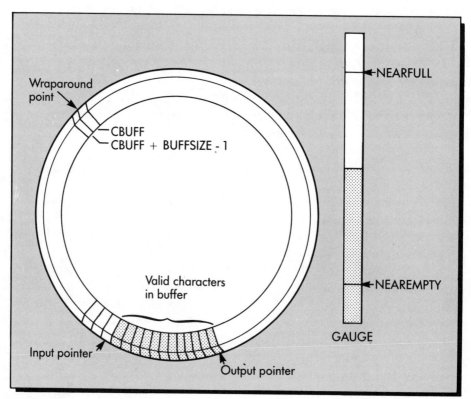

Figure 10-1. Circular buffer

should be some room beyond the cutoff point. The amount of extra room needed is dependent upon the particular situation. You can control this by adjusting NEARFULL. Once input is cut off and the buffer is sufficiently emptied out, there needs to be a way to resume the input. NEAREMPTY provides this limit.

The SAVE routine is actually a complete program to save files from one of the two communications lines to the disk. It calls the circular buffer routines mentioned above and is a good example of the use of such a buffer.

The last three routines CRFILTER, WSFILTER, and COUNT are designed to be *filters*. A filter is a program that reads data from a standard input device, modifies the data, and then writes it to a standard output device. Because I/O through a standard output device can be redirected, filters can be used to process files. In fact, this capability allows filters to be used as operators on files, providing the user with the ability to manipulate files with as much ease as numbers can be manipulated with arithmetic operations. This is useful in such applications as converting files from one format to another and extracting information from files.

CRFILTER strips off bit 7 from each byte, adds linefeeds to carriage returns, and expands tabs. This is a handy combination of operations and can be used for such purposes as making certain external file formats are compatible with certain editors such as WordStar, and making WordStar files compatible with DOS utilities. This program is meant to be a model that you can use to build your own reformatting filter.

WSFILTER replaces any single cr/lf with a "soft" cr/lf and any double cr/lf with a "soft" then a "hard" cr/lf. Tabs are not expanded. This is useful for converting text files from line-oriented editors that use "hard" carriage returns on each line of text to files that are compatible with editors such as WordStar which use "soft" carriage returns to help form temporary line terminators.

COUNT counts the number of characters and words in a file. It represents a type of filter in which information is abstracted or extracted from files. The SORT and FIND filters supplied with IBM PC DOS 2 also are of this type.

EMESSOUT

Exception Message Output

Function: This routine sends a specified exception message out through the standard output device.

Input: Upon entry AX contains the exception message number as listed in the table below. This table is an extension of the Error Return Table in the DOS 2 Disk Operating System manual.

Output: The output is sent to the standard output device.

Registers Used: AX is used for input.

Segments Referenced: Upon entry the data segment must contain the text of the exception messages as in the following table:

```
emess    dw      emess1
         dw      emess2
         dw      emess3
         dw      emess4
         dw      emess5
         dw      emess6
         dw      emess7
         dw      emess8
         dw      emess9
         dw      emess1Ø
         dw      emess11
         dw      emess12
         dw      emess13
         dw      emess14
         dw      emess15
         dw      emess16
         dw      emess17
         dw      emess18
;
emess1  db      cr,lf,'Invalid function number',cr,lf,Ø
emess2  db      cr,lf,'File not found',cr,lf,Ø
emess3  db      cr,lf,'Path not found',cr,lf,Ø
emess4  db      cr,lf,'Too many open files',cr,lf,Ø
emess5  db      cr,lf,'Access denied',cr,lf,Ø
emess6  db      cr,lf,'Invalid handle',cr,lf,Ø
emess7  db      cr,lf,'Memory control blocks destroyed',cr,lf,Ø
emess8  db      cr,lf,'Insufficient memory',cr,lf,Ø
emess9  db      cr,lf,'Invalid memory block address',cr,lf,Ø
emess1Ø db      cr,lf,'Invalid environment',cr,lf,Ø
emess11 db      cr,lf,'Invalid format',cr,lf,Ø
```

```
ness12   db        cr,lf,'Invalid access code',cr,lf,Ø
ness13   db        cr,lf,'Invalid data',cr,lf,Ø
ness14   db        cr,lf,'Message not in use',lf,Ø
ness15   db        cr,lf,'Invalid drive was specified',cr,lf,Ø
ness16   db        cr,lf,'Attempted to remove the current directory',cr,lf,Ø
ness17   db        cr,lf,'Not same device',cr,lf,Ø
ness18   db        cr,lf,'No more files',cr,lf,Ø
```

The first part of the table consists of addresses of the messages and the second part consists of the actual messages as ASCIIZ strings.

Routines Called: MESSOUT

Special Notes: None.

```
ROUTINE TO SEND OUT EXCEPTION MESSAGES

messout          proc    far

        push    si              ; save registers
        push    ax

        add     ax,ax           ; double to index through table
        mov     si,ax           ; SI points into table
        mov     si,emess[si]    ; look up address of message
        call    messout         ; send the message

        pop     ax              ; restore registers
        pop     si
        ret

messout          endp
```

GETSPEC

Get a File Specifier

Function: This routine gets a file specifier from the unformatted parameter area at 80h of the Program Segment Prefix and transfers it to an ASCIIZ buffer. When you enter a transient command, the DOS automatically fills the unformatted parameter area with the tail of the command line.

Input: Upon entry, the unformatted parameter area must contain a file specifier and DS:DX must point to a buffer in memory.

Output: The buffer is filled with the file specification as an ASCIIZ string.

Registers Used: No registers are modified. DX is used for input.

Segments Referenced: Upon entry the extra segment must contain the ASCIIZ string buffer.

Routines Called: None.

Special Notes: The double word variable DTA must point to the default DTA in the Program Segment Prefix. In particular, the second word of this variable should be loaded with the Program Segment Prefix when the user first gains control. This segment value is initially contained in DS.

```
; ROUTINE TO GET A FILE SPECIFIER
;
getspec proc    far
;
        push    ds              ; save registers
        push    es
        push    si
        push    di
        push    cx
;
; set up pointer to dta to get parameters
        lds     si,dta          ; point to dta for parameters
        mov     cl,[si]         ; get length of string
        mov     ch,Ø            ; make 16-bit
        inc     si              ; skip the length byte
; scan past the spaces
        mov     al,' '          ; skip spaces
```

```
getspec1:
        cmp     [si],al         ; check for space
        jne     getspec2        ; exit the loop if nonspace
        inc     si              ; otherwise point to next byte
        loop    getspec1        ; loop back for more
        jcxz    getspec3        ; no file specifier?

; move the rest into place
getspec2:
        mov     di,dx           ; index points to destination
        cld                     ; forward direction
        rep     movsb           ; make the transfer
        clc                     ; no error so no carry
        jmp     getspecexit     ; and return

getspec3:
        mov     ax,20           ; no file specified
        stc                     ; set carry for error
        jmp     getspecexit     ; and exit

getspecexit:
        pop     cx              ; save registers
        pop     di
        pop     si
        pop     es
        pop     ds
        ret

getspec endp
```

CREATEFILE

Create a File

Function: This routine creates a file for read/write. If a file already exists, then its length is truncated to zero, ready to be written to.

Input: Upon entry DS:DX points to an ASCIIZ string with the drive, path, and filename.

Output: If the file can be opened, the carry is clear and its handle is returned in AX. If it cannot be opened, the carry is set and an error code is returned in AX.

Registers Used: Only AX is modified. DX is used for input and AX is used for output.

Segments Referenced: Upon entry the data segment must contain the ASCIIZ string.

Routines Called: DOS call number 3Ch (CREAT) is used.

Special Notes: None.

```
; ROUTINE TO CREATE A FILE
;
createfile      proc    far
;
        push    cx              ; save registers
;
        mov     cx,Ø            ; attribute Ø
        mov     ah,3Ch          ; create file
        int     21h             ; DOS call
;
        pop     cx              ; restore registers
        ret
;
createfile      endp
```

CLOSEFILE

Close a File

Function: This routine closes a file.

Input: Upon entry BX contains the file handle of the file that is to be closed.

Output: If the file can be closed, the carry is clear. If it cannot be closed, the carry is set and an error code is returned in AX.

Registers Used: Only AX is modified. BX is used for input and AX is used for output.

Segments Referenced: None.

Routines Called: DOS call number 3Eh (close file) is used.

Special Notes: None.

```
ROUTINE TO CLOSE A FILE

losefile        proc    far

        mov     ah,3Eh          ; close a file
        int     21h             ; DOS call
        ret

losefile        endp
```

WRITEFILE

Write Bytes to a File

Function: This routine writes bytes to a file.

Input: Upon entry BX contains the file's handle, DS:DX points to a linear buffer containing the bytes, and CX contains the byte count.

Output: If the bytes are successfully written to the file, the carry is clear, and if it is not, the carry is set and the error code is in AX.

Registers Used: No registers are modified. AX and BX are used for input and AX is used for output.

Segments Referenced: The data segment must contain the linear byte buffer LBUFF.

Routines Called: DOS call number 40h (write to a file) is used.

Special Notes: None.

```
; ROUTINE TO WRITE A BYTE TO A FILE
;
writefile       proc    far
;
        mov     ah,40h          ; write to file
        int     21h             ; DOS call
        cmp     ax,cx           ; was it all written?
        je      writefile1      ; skip if ok
        mov     ax,21           ; not all bytes were transferred
        stc                     ; set carry if error
;
writefile1:
        ret
;
writefile       endp
```

READFILE

Read Bytes from a File

Function: This routine reads bytes from a file.

Input: Upon entry BX contains the file's handle, CX contains the count, and DS:DX points to a linear buffer where the bytes are to appear.

Output: If the bytes are successfully read from the file, the carry is clear, and if it is not, the carry is set and the error code is returned in AL.

Registers Used: No registers are modified. CX, DX, and BX are used for input.

Segments Referenced: The data segment must contain the linear byte buffer LBUFF.

Routines Called: DOS call number 3Fh (read from a file) is used.

Special Notes: None.

```
; ROUTINE TO READ BYTES FROM A FILE
;
readfile        proc    far
;
        mov     ah,3Fh          ; read from a file
        int     21h             ; DOS call
;
        cmp     ax,cx           ; everything back?
        je      readfileexit    ; skip if ok
        mov     ax,22           ; not all read
        stc                     ; set carry for error
;
readfileexit:
        ret
;
readfile        endp
```

INITCBUFF

Initialize Circular Buffer

Function: This routine initializes the pointers and control variables for a circular buffer.

Input: None.

Output: The registers SI and DI and the variable GAUGE are all set to zero. The variable LASTBYTE is also set equal to zero.

Registers Used: DI and SI are set to zero. All other registers are left alone.

Segments Referenced: Upon entry the data segment must contain the circular buffer and its variables, CBUFF and GAUGE, and the variable LASTBYTE.

Routines Called: None.

Special Notes: None.

```
; ROUTINE TO HANDLE INPUT FOR CIRCULAR BUFFER
;
initcbuff       proc    far
;
        mov     si,Ø            ; initialize SI
        mov     di,Ø            ; initialize DI
        mov     gauge,Ø         ; and number of bytes in buffer
        mov     lastbyte,Ø      ; also last byte buffer
;
        ret
;
initcbuff       endp
```

PUTCBUFF

Put a Byte into Circular Buffer

Function: This routine puts one byte into a circular buffer.

Input: Upon entry a byte is in AL.

Output: The byte goes into the circular buffer. The pointers and gauge variables are properly adjusted. If the buffer gets nearly full then a routine is called to send a signal to the communications device to stop sending any more bytes of output.

Registers Used: DI is the buffer pointer and is updated if there is a character.

Segments Referenced: Upon entry the data segment must contain the circular buffer and its variables, CBUFF and GAUGE, and the variable LASTBYTE.

Routines Called: COMOFF

Special Notes: None.

```
ROUTINE TO PUT ONE BYTE INTO A CIRCULAR BUFFER

utcbuff         proc    far

put the byte into the buffer
        mov     cbuff[di],al    ; byte goes into buffer

adjust pointer
        inc     di              ; point to next character
        cmp     di,cbuffsize    ; wrap it around?
        jne     putcbuff1       ; skip if no wrap
        mov     di,∅            ; wraps back to zero

count it
utcbuff1:
        inc     gauge           ; count the character
        cmp     gauge,nearfull  ; too many characters?
        jne     putcbuff2       ; skip if not
        call    comoff          ; request to stop flow
```

```
putcbuff2:
;
putcbuffret:
        ret
;
putcbuff        endp
```

INCBUFF

Input to Circular Buffer

Function: This routine handles input to a circular buffer. It checks to see if there is any input from a serial communications line. If there is input then it is sent to a circular buffer. If a control Z is received then carry is set and an exception code is returned. If there is no input then it returns with the carry clear and without further action.

Input: Upon entry DX specifies the communications line (0 = com1: and 1 = com2:). During the routine input is from COMINCK routine.

Output: The input characters go to the circular buffer. If the buffer gets nearly full then a routine is called to send a signal to the communications device to stop sending any more bytes of output. If a control Z is detected from the communications line the carry is set and an exception code is returned.

Registers Used: DI is the buffer pointer and is updated if there is a character.

Segments Referenced: Upon entry the data segment must contain the circular buffer and its variables, CBUFF and GAUGE, and the variable LASTBYTE.

Routines Called: COMON, COMOFF, COMINCK, PUTCBUFF

Special Notes: None.

```
ROUTINE TO HANDLE INPUT FOR CIRCULAR BUFFER

incbuff proc    far

check for a character
        call    cominck         ; check for character
        jz      incbuffexit     ; good exit if none

strip off parity bit
        and     al,7Fh          ; just 7 bits

check for linefeed
        cmp     al,1Ø           ; ASCII 1Ø is linefeed
        jne     incbuff1        ; skip if not linefeed
```

```
                cmp     lastbyte,13     ; was last byte a carriage return?
                je      incbuff2        ; skip if cr/lf
;
incbuff1:
                call    putcbuff        ; put byte into buffer
                mov     lastbyte,al     ; update last byte
;
; check for carriage return and
incbuff2:
                cmp     al,13           ; ASCII 13 is carriage return
                jne     incbuff3        ; skip if not
;
; also put a linefeed if character was a carriage return
                push    ax              ; save current character
                mov     al,10           ; put a linefeed
                call    putcbuff        ; into buffer
                pop     ax              ; restore current character
;
; check for end of file
incbuff3:
                cmp     al,controlz     ; end of file?
                je      incbuff5        ; is an exception
;
; check for overflow
                cmp     gauge,nearfull  ; too many characters?
                jl      incbuff4        ; skip if not
                call    comoff          ; request to stop flow
                jmp     incbuffexit     ; good exit
;
; if not overflow make sure flow is on
incbuff4:
                call    comon           ; make sure flow is on
                jmp     incbuffexit     ; good exit
;
; handle end of file exception
incbuff5:
                mov     ax,19           ; end of file code
                stc                     ; set carry for error
                jmp     incbuffret      ; return with error
;
incbuffexit:
                clc                     ; clear carry - no error
;
incbuffret:
                ret
;
incbuff endp
```

FLUSHIT

Flush the Circular Buffer

Function: This routine flushes all bytes from a circular buffer, sending them to a specified file.

Input: Upon entry BX contains the file handle of the output file. During the routine, input is from the circular buffer.

Output: Output is to a file whose handle is in BX.

Registers Used: Only AX and SI are modified. AX contains the exception code, SI is the buffer pointer and is updated to reflect the characters taken. BX is the file handle for the output file.

Segments Referenced: Upon entry the data segment must contain the circular buffer and its variables, CBUFF and GAUGE, the variable LASTBYTE, and the linear buffer LBUFF.

Routines Called: WRITEFILE

Special Notes: None.

```
; ROUTINE TO FLUSH A CIRCULAR BUFFER
;
flushit proc     far
;
        push    di              ; save registers
        push    dx
        push    cx
;
; get the bytes from the buffer
        mov     cx,gauge        ; get the count
        jcxz    flushitexit     ; check for empty
        mov     di,∅            ; initialize destination
;
; loop to get all the bytes
flushit1:
        mov     al,cbuff[si]    ; get the character
        inc     si              ; increment the pointer
        cmp     si,cbuffsize    ; wrap it?
        jne     flushit2        ; skip if no wrap ·
        mov     si,∅            ; wrap the buffer pointer
```

```
flushit2:
        mov     lbuff[di],al    ; put the byte in linear buffer
        inc     di
        loop    flushit1        ; loop until all bytes in lbuff
;
; send the linear buffer to the disk
        mov     cx,gauge        ; this is the number of bytes
        lea     dx,lbuff        ; this is where they are
        call    writefile       ; send them out
        mov     gauge,Ø         ; set circular buffer empty
;
flushitexit:
        pop     cx              ; restore registers
        pop     dx
        pop     di
        ret
;
flushit endp
```

OUTCBUFF

Output from Circular Buffer

Function: This routine handles output from a circular buffer. It checks to see if there are enough bytes in the buffer to send to disk. If there are not enough then it returns without further action. If there are enough then it sends a block of bytes to an opened file through the WRITEFILE routine.

Input: Upon entry BX contains the file handle of the output file. Input is from the circular buffer.

Output: Output is to a file. If the buffer gets nearly empty then a control Q is sent to the standard output device. If the write was unsuccessful the carry is set and the error code is returned. If a control Z is detected from the circular buffer the carry is set and error code 19 (end of file) is returned.

Registers Used: Only AX and SI are modified. AX contains the exception code, SI is the buffer pointer and is updated according to the characters taken. BX is the file handle for the output file.

Segments Referenced: Upon entry the data segment must contain the circular buffer and its variables, CBUFF and GAUGE, and the variable LASTBYTE.

Routines Called: COMOFF, FLUSHIT

Special Notes: None

```
ROUTINE TO HANDLE OUTPUT FROM A CIRCULAR BUFFER

utcbuff        proc    far

check for enough characters in the buffer
        cmp     gauge,blksize   ; any characters?
        jl      outcbuffexit    ; exit if no characters

empty the buffer
        call    comoff          ; hold the com line
        call    flushit         ; flush the buffer
        jc      outcbuffret     ; error?
```

```
;
outcbuffexit:
        clc     ; clear carry - no exception
outcbuffret:
        ret
;
outcbuff        endp
```

SAVE

Save a File from Communications Line to Disk

Function: This routine saves a file from a communications line to a disk file.

Input: Upon entry the file specifier is in the unformatted parameter area of the program segment prefix. This contains the tail of the command line which invoked the SAVE command. During the routine input is from the communications line which in this case is com2: initialized as 2400 baud, even parity, 8-bit data word, and one stop bit.

Output: The output is sent to the disk file.

Registers Used: Registers are used as needed. This is the main program of an EXE command file.

Segments Referenced: Upon entry the segments must be as for entry to EXE files.

Routines Called: GETSPEC, CREATEFILE, CLOSEFILE, INITCBUFF, INCBUFF, OUTCBUFF, COMINIT, COMON, EMESSOUT

Special Notes: None

```
        extrn    stdinck:far
        extrn    emessout:far,getspec:far
        extrn    createfile:far,closefile:far
        extrn    cominit:far,comon:far,comoff:far
        extrn    initcbuff:far,incbuff:far,outcbuff:far
        extrn    flushit:far
        extrn    dta:dword

;
; *************************************************************
;
datas   segment public
;
namebuff         db      256 dup(∅)
;
datas   ends
```

```
; **********************************************************
stacks   segment stack
         db       20 dup('stack    ')
stacks   ends
; **********************************************************
codes    segment
;
         assume  cs:codes,ds:datas
;
; ROUTINE TO SAVE FILE FROM COMMUNICATION LINE TO DISK
;
save     proc    far
;
; set up return
         push    ds              ; save for proper return
         mov     ax,0            ; points to beginning of segment
         push    ax              ; for the offset
;
; set up segments
         mov     dx,ds           ; program segment prefix was data seg
         mov     ax,datas        ; new data segment
         mov     ds,ax           ; put in DS
         mov     es,ax           ; and in ES
         mov     dta+2,dx        ; set the segment of the data
;
; set up the file
         lea     dx,namebuff     ; point to ASCIIZ buffer
         call    getspec         ; get file specifications
         jc      exception       ; error?
         lea     dx,namebuff     ; ASCIIZ buffer has file specifiers
         call    createfile      ; set up the file
         jc      exception       ; error?
         mov     bx,ax           ; get the file handle
;
; set up the communications line
         mov     dx,1            ; for com2:
         mov     al,0BBh         ; 2400:e,8,1
         call    cominit         ; initialize it
         call    comon           ; turn it on
;
; initialize the buffer
         call    initcbuff       ; initialize the buffer
         mov     dx,1            ; com2:
;
; main loop for pulling in bytes
saveloop:
         call    incbuff         ; check for input
         jc      exception       ; error or end of file?
         call    outcbuff        ; check to send it out
```

```
        jc      exception       ; error?
        jmp     saveloop

; handle exceptions
exception:
        cmp     ax,19           ; end of file?
        je      save1           ; if so close it up and return

        call    emessout        ; report the error
        jmp     saveexit        ; and return

; normal return
save1:
        call    comoff          ; com line off
        call    flushit         ; flush the buffer
        jc      exception       ; error?
        call    closefile       ; close the file
        jc      exception       ; error?
        jmp     saveexit        ; exit

; common return
saveexit:
        call    comon           ; com line on
        ret

save    endp
codes   ends                    ; end of code segment
        end     save
```

CRFILTER

Filter For Carriage Return/Linefeed

Function: This routine filters a file, replacing carriage returns by carriage return/linefeeds. Tabs are expanded.

Input: Input is from the standard input device.

Output: The output is sent to the standard output device.

Registers Used: Registers are used as needed. This is the main program of an EXE command file.

Segments Referenced: Upon entry the segments must be as specified for entry to EXE files.

Routines Called: STDINNE, STDOUT

Special Notes: None

```
;
controlz          equ     1Ah       ; control Z
;
        extrn    stdinne:far,stdout:far
;
;***********************************************************
datas    segment public
;
lastbyte          db      Ø
;
datas    ends
;***********************************************************
stacks   segment stack
        db       2Ø dup('stack   ')
stacks   ends
;***********************************************************
codes    segment
;
        assume   cs:codes,ds:datas
;
; ROUTINE TO FILTER FILES FOR CARRIAGE RETURNS
;
crfilter          proc    far
;
; set up return
```

```
        push    ds              ; save for proper return
        mov     ax,Ø            ; points to beginning of segment
        push    ax              ; for the offset

set up segments
        mov     ax,datas        ; new data segment
        mov     ds,ax           ; put in DS
        mov     es,ax           ; and in ES

main loop
rfilter1:

get the next character
        call    stdinne         ; get the character without echo

strip off bit 7
        and     al,7Fh          ; just 7 bits

check for linefeed
        cmp     al,1Ø           ; ASCII 1Ø
        jne     crfilter2       ; skip if not linefeed
        cmp     lastbyte,13     ; was last byte a carriage return?
        je      crfilter3       ; skip if cr/lf

rfilter2:
        call    stdout          ; send it out
        mov     lastbyte,al     ; update last byte

check for carriage return
rfilter3:
        cmp     al,13           ; ASCII 13
        jne     crfilter4       ; skip if so

        push    ax              ; save current character
        mov     al,1Ø           ; put a linefeed
        call    stdout          ; out the standard output
        pop     ax              ; restore current character

check for end of file
rfilter4:
        cmp     al,controlz     ; end of file?
        jne     crfilter1       ; if not, back for more

exit
rfilterexit:
        ret

rfilter          endp
odes     ends                   ; end of code segment
        end     crfilter
```

WSFILTER

Filter to Help Convert Files to WordStar Format

Function: This routine filters a file, replacing any single cr/lf by a "soft" cr/lf and any double cr/lf by a "soft" then a "hard" cr/lf. Tabs are not expanded.

Input: Input is from the standard input device.

Output: The output is sent to the standard output device.

Registers Used: Registers are used as needed. This is the main program of an EXE command file.

Segments Referenced: Upon entry the segments must be as specified for entry to EXE files.

Routines Called: STDINNE, STDOUTDR

Special Notes: None

```
;
controlz        equ     1Ah     ; control Z
;
        extrn   stdinne:far,stdoutdr:far
;
;*************************************************************
datas   segment public
;
lastbyte        db      Ø
;
datas   ends
;*************************************************************
stacks  segment stack
        db      2Ø dup('stack   ')
stacks  ends
;*************************************************************
codes   segment
;
        assume  cs:codes,ds:datas
;
; ROUTINE TO HELP CONVERT FILES TO WORDSTAR FILES
;
wsfilter        proc    far
```

```
      set up return
            push      ds              ; save for proper return
            mov       ax,Ø            ; points to beginning of segment
            push      ax              ; for the offset

      set up segments
            mov       ax,datas        ; new data segment
            mov       ds,ax           ; put in DS
            mov       es,ax           ; and in ES

      main loop
sfilter1:

      get the next character
            call      stdinne         ; get the character without echo

      work on carriage returns
sfilter2:
            cmp       al,ØDh          ; hard carriage return
            jne       wsfilter3       ; skip if not
            cmp       lastbyte,1Ø     ; last character = linefeed?
            je        wsfilter3       ; skip if so
            mov       al,8Dh          ; soft carriage return

      send the character out
sfilter3:
            call      stdoutdr        ; send it out
            mov       lastbyte,al     ; update last byte

      check for end of file
            cmp       al,controlz     ; end of file?
            jne       wsfilter1       ; if not, back for more

      exit
sfilterexit:
            ret

sfilter          endp
odes   ends                           ; end of code segment
            end       wsfilter
```

COUNT

Filter to Count Words and Characters in a File

Function: This routine counts the words and characters in a file. It can be used as a filter.

Input: Input is from the standard input device.

Output: The output is sent to the standard output device.

Registers Used: Registers are used as needed. This is the main program of an EXE command file.

Segments Referenced: Upon entry the segments must be as specified for entry to EXE files.

Routines Called: STDINNE, STDOUT

Special Notes: None

```
;
lf              equ     1Ø
cr              equ     13
;
controlz        equ     1Ah        ; control Z
;
        extrn   stdinne:far,stdout:far,stdcrlf:far
        extrn   stdmessout:far
        extrn   dec16out:far
;
; **********************************************************
datas   segment public
;
; VARIABLES FOR COUNTING
;
charcount       dw      Ø
wordcount       dw      Ø
state           db      Ø
;
; MESSAGES
;
charmess        db      'characters: ',Ø
wordmess        db      'words:      ',Ø
;
datas   ends
```

```
************************************************************
stacks   segment stack
         db       20 dup('stack   ')
stacks   ends
************************************************************
codes    segment

         assume   cs:codes,ds:datas

LOCAL SUBROUTINE TO CHECK FOR ALPHANUMERICS

Input: Upon entry ASCII code in AL
Output: Upon exit CY = not alphanumeric
                  NC = alphanumeric

alphanum         proc     near

         push     ax              ; save registers

         and      al,7Fh          ; strip off bit 7
         cmp      al,'1'          ; below '1'?
         jb       alphanum1       ; not alphanumeric

         cmp      al,'9'          ; from '1' to '9'?
         jbe      alphanum2       ; yes it's ok

         cmp      al,'A'          ; below 'A'?
         jb       alphanum1       ; not alphanumeric

         cmp      al,'Z'          ; from 'A' to 'Z'?
         jbe      alphanum2       ; yes it's ok

         cmp      al,'a'          ; below 'a'?
         jb       alphanum1       ; not alphanumeric

         cmp      al,'z'          ; from 'a' to 'z'?
         jbe      alphanum2       ; yes it's ok

         jmp      alphanum1       ; above 'z' is not alphanumeric
;
alphanum1:
         stc                      ; not alphanumeric
         jmp      alphanumexit
alphanum2:
         clc                      ; yes it's alphanumeric
         jmp      alphanumexit
;
alphanumexit:
         pop      ax              ; restore registers
         ret
```

```
;
alphanum        endp
;
;
;
;  ROUTINE TO COUNT WORDS AND CHARACTERS IN A FILE
;
count   proc    far
;
        push    ds              ; save for proper return
        mov     ax,Ø            ; points to beginning of segment
        push    ax              ; for the offset
;
        mov     ax,datas        ; new data segment
        mov     ds,ax           ; put in DS
        mov     es,ax           ; and in ES
;
;  initialize the counts and state
        mov     charcount,Ø     ; set character count to zero
        mov     wordcount,Ø     ; set word count to zero
        mov     state,Ø         ; and alphanumeric state too
;
;  main loop
count1:
;
;  get the next character
        call    stdinne         ; get the character without echo
        inc     charcount       ; count the character
;
;  check for end of file
        cmp     al,controlz     ; end of file?
        jne     count2          ; skip if not
        jmp     countexit       ; exit if control Z is found
;
;  check for alphanumeric
count2:
        call    alphanum        ; check for alphanumeric
        jc      count4          ; not alphanumeric
;
;  current character is alphanumeric
count3:
        mov     al,1            ; current state is alphanumeric
        xchg    state,al        ; update state and get new state
        cmp     al,Ø            ; state change?
        jne     count5          ; skip if not
        inc     wordcount       ; count it if so
        jmp     count5
;
;  current character is nonalphanumeric
count4:
        mov     state,Ø         ; current state is nonalphanumeric
```

```
ount5:
        jmp     count1          ; loop back for next byte

ountexit:

; report number of characters
        lea     si,charmess
        call    stdmessout
        mov     dx,charcount
        call    dec16out
        call    stdcrlf

; report number of words
        lea     si,wordmess
        call    stdmessout
        mov     dx,wordcount
        call    dec16out
        call    stdcrlf

; return
        ret

ount    endp
odes    ends                    ; end of code segment
        end     count
```

Index